The Complete Project Manager's

Toolkit

D1088294

The Complete Project Manager's

Toolkit

Randall L. Englund

Alfonso Bucero

MANAGEMENTCONCEPTSPRESS

MANAGEMENTCONCEPTSPRESS

8230 Leesburg Pike, Suite 800
Tysons Corner, VA 22182
(703) 790-9595
Fax: (703) 790-1371
www.managementconcepts.com

Copyright © 2012 by Management Concepts, Inc.

All rights reserved. No part of this book may be reproduced or utilized in any form or by any means, electronic or mechanical, including photocopying, recording, or by an information storage and retrieval system, without permission in writing from the publisher, except for brief quotations in review articles.

Printed in the United States of America

978-1-56726-360-2

10   9   8   7   6   5   4   3   2   1

ABOUT THE AUTHORS

Randall L. Englund, MBA, BSEE, NPDP, CBM, is an author, speaker, trainer, professional facilitator, and founder, principal, and executive consultant for the Englund Project Management Consultancy (www .englundpmc.com). He also facilitates project management seminars for the Project Management Institute and conducts courses at University of California extensions and for other professional associations.

Randy draws upon experiences as a former senior project manager with Hewlett-Packard Company (HP) for 22 years. In a corporate project management initiative, he led the continuous improvement of project management across the company and documented best practices in *ActionSheets*; in business units, he released high-technology products, developed a system life cycle, resolved architectural issues, researched effective practices for project success, and designed management processes, courses, and distance learning. Prior to working with HP, he served as a field service engineer and installation supervisor for GE Medical Systems.

He has an MBA degree in management from San Francisco State University and a BS in electrical engineering from the University of California, Santa Barbara. He is a member of the Project Management Institute and the American Management Association and is a former board member for the Product Development and Management Association (PDMA), where he is a certified New Product Development Professional (NPDP). Randy is a Certified Business Manager (CBM) with the Association for Professionals in Business Management.

With Dr. Robert J. Graham, he coauthored the books *Creating an Environment for Successful Projects: Second Edition* (2004) and *Creating the Project Office: A Manager's Guide to Leading Organizational Change* (2003). With Alfonso Bucero, he coauthored *Project Sponsorship: Achieving Management Commitment for Project Success* (2006).

In his work around the world, Randy provides management and leadership awareness at a systemic and organic level through multimedia presentations, workshops, conference papers, and writings. In addition to his own books and articles in magazines, he has contributed chapters in books such as the *AMA Handbook of Project Management: Third Edition* (2010), *Advising Upwards* (2011), and *Organizational Project Management* (2010). His interactive style encourages the exploration of action-oriented practices that are immediately applicable to optimizing results from project-based work.

Alfonso Bucero, MSc, PMP (Project Management Professional), is the founder and managing partner of BUCERO PM Consulting (www.abucero.com). He managed IIL Spain for almost two years, and he was a senior project manager at Hewlett-Packard Spain (Madrid office) for thirteen years.

Alfonso is a member of PMI, ALI (Asociación de Licenciados, Ingenieros y Doctores en Informática), AEIPRO (an International Project Management Association member organization) and a DINTEL advisor. Alfonso was the founder, sponsor, and former president of PMI Barcelona, Spain, Chapter, and he is an IPMA Assessor. He was a member of the Congress Project Action Team of PMI EMEA's Congresses in Edinburgh, Madrid, and Budapest. He graduated from PMI's Leadership Institute Master Class 2007. He served as president of the PMI Madrid, Spain, chapter and serves as Component Mentor for Region 8 South. He received the PMI Distinguished Contribution Award in 2010 for his long and varied body of work. In 2011, Alfonso received PMI's Fellow of the Institute award, intended to recognize and honor PMI members who have made sustained and significant contributions to PMI and the project management profession for more than a decade. It is PMI's highest and most prestigious award presented to an individual.

Alfonso has a degree in computer science engineering from Universidad Politécnica (Madrid) and is a Ph.D. candidate in project management at the University of Zaragoza in Spain. He has 27 years of practical experience, 22 of them in project management worldwide. He has managed and consulted on projects in various countries across Europe.

Since 1994, Alfonso has been a frequent speaker at international PMI Congresses and SeminarsWorld. He delivers PM training and consulting services in countries across the globe. As a "project management believer," he asserts that *passion, persistence,* and *patience* are vital keys for project success.

He authored the book *Dirección de Proyectos, Una Nueva Vision* (2003). He contributed Chapter 7 of *Creating the Project Office* (2003), authored by Randall L. Englund, Robert J. Graham, and Paul Dinsmore. He coauthored the chapter "From Commander to Sponsor: Building Executive Support for Project Success" in the book *Advising Upwards* (2011).

Alfonso coauthored with Randall L. Englund the book *Project Sponsorship* (2006) and authored *Today Is a Good Day: Attitudes for Achieving Project Success* (2010). He has also contributed to professional magazines in the U.S., Russia (SOVNET), India (ICFAI), Argentina, and Spain. Alfonso is a contributing editor of the "Crossing Borders" column in *PM Network*, published by the Project Management Institute. BUCERO PM Consulting is a Registered Education Provider (REP) with PMI.

CONTENTS

Preface xi

Introduction xv

Chapter 1   Leadership and Management Skills 1

Chapter 2   The Role of Humor and Fun 33

Chapter 3   Personal Skills 43

Chapter 4   Project Management Skills 73

Chapter 5   Environment Skills 93

Chapter 6   Organization Skills 119

Chapter 7   Negotiating Skills 131

Chapter 8   Political Skills 147

Chapter 9   Conflict Management Skills 159

Chapter 10   Sales Skills 167

Chapter 11   Change Management Skills 175

Chapter 12   Market and Customer Knowledge 185

Appendix 197

References and Resources 201

PREFACE

The Complete Project Manager integrates key technical, people, business, and organizational skills. This companion to the core book offers related tools, checklists, tables, and examples.

The core book establishes the premise that success in any environment largely depends on completing successful projects, and successful projects get done by skilled project managers and teams, supported by effective project sponsors. It is the integration across a spectrum of skills that enables certain individuals to make a difference and achieve more optimized outcomes. The ultimate aim of this book is to put action-oriented tools into your hands, allowing you to develop a complete set of skills that is the right set for you to excel in today's competitive environment. The goal is to equip you and your colleagues to be leaders and managers in the project environment... and beyond.

INTENDED AUDIENCES

As with the core book, the primary audience is project, program, and portfolio managers, in all disciplines and industries, commercial, nonprofit, and government. You may be new to the profession and be seeking a primer to get started in the right direction. You may have a few years of experience and want to get on a fast track. You may have lots of experience but have come to realize that a fresh start and changed thinking are on the agenda, perhaps triggered by layoffs, job changes, or other transitions. This audience is huge—note that there are more than 350,000 members of the Project Management Institute across the globe.

The secondary audience is individual contributors, subject matter experts (SMEs), project team members, managers of project managers, project sponsors, and other executives. They may be new to this role and wonder what they are getting into—how can they better understand the people, roles, and expectations for the people they work with? Or they may be experienced and looking for leading practices that accelerate their performance. This audience is even larger than the number of project managers. We hope your experience with this book prompts you to share it with this extended audience.

PURPOSE AND USES

This *Toolkit* is designed to put tools in your hands that will help you implement the concepts we cover. The concepts are simple to understand, universal, powerful, and immediately applicable. You may already be aware of *what* you need to do but, for any number of reasons, you are not doing it. This book supplies the *how*. It provides checklists, tables, and examples from real people of how to apply the concepts, thereby demonstrating their feasibility. It removes barriers to implementation. These barriers may be environmental, executive, or business-related—anything that has seemed like an obstacle and that has delayed projects, caused cost overruns, lowered quality, or caused deliverables to not meet requirements. These barriers existed because people were not aligned and motivated to perform. To overcome them, you may just need to see a model for how a task or process can be implemented. The *Toolkit* and the core book will expose you to implementation aids and show you complete ways to look at your situation and see new solutions or apply old solutions in new ways. The goal is to integrate knowledge and skills that make the difference in achieving optimized outcomes, increased satisfaction, and bottom-line results.

By reading this and the core book, you will discover evidence and examples for implementing a complete systems approach to project leadership. You will learn how soft skills applied to project management, environmental, leadership, negotiating, and persuasive skills can be creatively applied. You can achieve greater results through changed thinking and by using the simple, immediately actionable tools we provide. There is no complicated model to understand before applying the ideas and tools in this book.

The core book and this *Toolkit* may be used as self-study; they may serve as references that you come back to repeatedly to refresh your thinking or find new insights; they may be used by book clubs to trigger sharing of similar or different experiences; they may be used by universities and training companies in the ever-growing number of courses offered on management and leadership; and they may be used by the authors and other consultants in seminars they facilitate worldwide.

Key objectives we anticipate for readers of this *Toolkit* are to:

- Change your thinking about how to learn and apply necessary skills to enhance on-the-job performance
- Apply different approaches to leading and managing projects, based upon examples and checklists
- Realize what needs to be done to achieve better results…and how to do it
- Further develop professional careers in project or program management.

Randall L. Englund
Burlingame, California USA
www.englundpmc.com

Alfonso Bucero
Madrid, Spain
www.abucero.com

February 2012

INTRODUCTION

Project Management Institute CEO Mark Langley writes, "It's not enough for project and program managers to have technical skills. We need leadership, conflict resolution and negotiation skills. Organizations are telling us, 'We're looking for the next business leaders.' And I say, 'It's about time'" (2011, p. 10).

While many professionals develop their craft through advanced education and on-the-job experiences, there comes a time when an enhanced skill set and a new perspective about working with people is necessary in order to advance to the next level of performance. How do you move beyond this plateau?

This *Toolkit* covers what it takes to be that next leader—a complete project manager. The goal is to integrate technical, people, and organization skills. The way to do this is to identify requisite skill sets and then learn from others about successful ways to develop and apply them. It is the integration of a spectrum of skills that enables certain individuals to make a difference and achieve more optimized outcomes. The ultimate aim is to develop a complete set of skills that is the right set to excel in today's competitive environment.

Each chapter within *The Complete Project Manager Toolkit* provides a set of standalone tools regarding a skill that is important in becoming a complete project manager. Of course, the real value is in integrating and using as many of the tools as possible.

Throughout this and the core companion book, we emphasize the importance of the project manager's having a positive attitude and how that approach helps organizations achieve project success. The key concept is that a variety of skills need to be integrated and applied in order to achieve optimized outcomes.

Use the molecule illustration in Figure I-1 to assess your skills in each of the twelve areas covered by this book. Initially rate yourself on a scale of one to seven, with a rating of one being very poor and seven very extraordinary. Do the assessment again after reading the book to validate your strengths and development opportunities and to reflect on your increased understanding from the journey through this material. Come back to the assessment periodically to monitor progress.

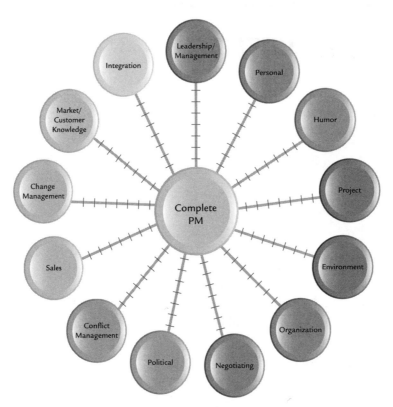

FIGURE I-1:   Molecular Assessment

Much as the field of chemistry offers an ever-increasing understanding of molecular structure, a robust set of project, program, and portfolio management skills provides the leadership to fuse disparate groups into new organizations. These new organizations may come about through organic growth or mergers, or by leadership that opens the way to novel or innovative solutions or new markets. Developments in combining molecules into increasingly more dense and complex structures allow for more potent outcomes in small packages, such as in prescription medicines. Likewise, project managers who develop more robust skill sets also become more potent and produce more effective outcomes within their organizations.

Unlimited combinations are possible for the "molecules" that compose complete project managers. There are many ways to assemble successful outcomes based on additional skill sets. New possibilities will emerge as skills are combined in different ways. The profession of project, program, and portfolio management will truly benefit from new developments among the people inhabiting its space.

 Drawing from nature's bounty, the dragonfly provides apt symbology for the complete project manager. For our purposes, the dragonfly symbolizes change, specifically changes in perspective and self-realization. This kind of change comes from mental and emotional maturity and working toward understanding how people work together in organizations.

The dragonfly's ability to scurry across water represents going beyond what's on the surface, exploring deeper implications and aspects of life. It moves with the utmost simplicity, effectiveness, and power, as well as elegance and grace. It can see all 360 degrees around it, symbolizing being able to see beyond the mundane and capture a wider picture of reality (Dragonfly Site n.d.).

This *Toolkit* opens doors by sharing the means to advance the efficacy of individual, team, and organizational performance. Infinite skill combinations are possible for the complete project manager. Achieving completeness is an unending journey. So let's get started…

LEADERSHIP AND MANAGEMENT SKILLS

TOOLSET: LEADING YOURSELF CHECKLIST

Nothing will make a better impression on your leader than your ability to manage yourself. If your leader must continually expend energy managing you, then you will be perceived as someone who drains time and energy. If you manage yourself well, however, your boss will see you as someone who maximizes opportunities and leverages personal strengths. That will make you someone your leader turns to when the heat is on.

Table 1-1 suggests ways to lead yourself well.

TABLE 1-1: Leading Yourself

What to Do	How to Do It
Manage your emotions	It is especially critical to control your emotions because whatever you do affects many other people. Good leaders know when to display emotions and when to delay expressing them. The bottom line in managing your emotions is that you should put others first—not yourself. Ask yourself, what does the team need? What also makes *me* feel better?
Manage your time	Time management issues are especially tough for people in the middle. Time is valuable. Until you value yourself, you won't value your time. Until you value your time, you will not do anything valuable with it. Instead of thinking about what you do and what you buy in terms of money, instead think about them in terms of time.

Manage your priorities	Get yourself to the point where you can manage your priorities and focus your time in this way: • 80% of the time, work where you are strongest. • 15% of the time, work where you are learning. • 5% of the time, work in other necessary areas. If you have people working for you, delegate to them tasks you are not good at but they are. The secret to making this shift is often discipline. Be ruthless in your judgment of what you should not do. Just because you like doing something does not mean it should stay on your to-do list. If a task is related to one of your strengths, do it. If it helps you grow, do it. If your leader says you must handle it personally, do it. Anything else is a candidate for your "stop doing" list.
Manage your energy	Some people have to ration their energy so that they don't run out. Always make sure you have the energy to do tasks with focus and excellence. Even people with high energy can have that energy sucked right out of them under difficult circumstances. Leaders, especially those in the middle of an organization, often have to deal with the "ABC energy drain": • Activity without direction: doing things that don't seem to matter • Burden without action: not being able to do things that really matter • Conflict without resolution: not being able to deal with what's the matter If you find that you are in an organization where you often must deal with these ABCs, then you will have to work extra hard to manage your energy well.
Manage your thinking	The greatest enemy of good thinking is busyness. And leaders in the middle are usually the busiest people in an organization. If you find that the pace of life is too demanding for you to stop and think during your workday, then get into the habit of jotting down three or four things that need good mental processing or planning that you cannot stop to think about. Then carve out some time later when you can give those items some good think-time. That may be 30 minutes at home the same day, or you may want to keep a running list for a whole week and then take a couple of hours on Saturday. Just don't let the list get so long that it disheartens or intimidates you.

TOOLSET: DELEGATING EFFECTIVELY

Don't take on tasks that someone else can do as well—or better—than you. Although a project manager cannot delegate everything in a project, delegating can make a project manager's life easier. But many are hesitant to pass on responsibilities.

Don't think of delegating as doing the other person a favor. Delegating some of your authority only makes *your* work easier. You will have more time to manage your project, monitor team members, and handle conflicts. Your organization will benefit, too, as output goes up and project work is completed more efficiently.

Communication is the key to delegating. Without communication, assignments are blurred, deadlines are vague, and results are, predictably, poor. If you want your team to excel as they take on added duties, talk to them, recognize them, and reward them.

To delegate effectively, follow these steps:

What To Do	How To Do It
Outline the purpose and importance of the project	Don't expect your team members to ask enough questions to define the project. Be sure to explain the work clearly and thoroughly.
Provide the necessary authority	Make sure the team member you have chosen has the clout needed to complete the task. Otherwise, requests to others for help and information may be ignored because they don't come from you.
Delegate for results	Set standards and make sure team members know they will be held accountable. When a problem arises, use it as a chance to show a staffer how to handle it.
Review and follow up	Setting deadlines and enforcing them will establish team members' commitment to getting the work done.

To make sure you are delegating to the right person, consider these factors:

1. **Friction:** Disagreement between you and the person taking the assignment is healthy while the assignment is being made. It is only a problem if it extends into the execution stage.

2. **Track record:** Match the job to the person. Past performance is significant only as it relates to the job you're delegating.

3. **Location:** Don't delegate just because someone is close by or is not busy and is convenient to ask.

4. **Organization level:** If you want to delegate a job to someone several levels down in the organization, first confer with his or her supervisors and explain the situation.

5. **Compatibility:** Ideally, your work and communication styles and that of the person to whom you are delegating the work should be complementary.

TOOLSET: 21ST-CENTURY LEADER QUALITIES ASSESSMENT

This tool helps you to assess your qualities as a leader. There are 21 characteristics to be assessed. Carefully select the number on the right that represents your present situation.

The codes to use are as follows:

1 = Never   **2** = Rarely   **3** = Sometimes   **4** = Frequently   **5** = All the time or daily

1. CHARACTER

1.	Do you think character is more than talk?	1 2 3 4 5
2.	Is character a choice for you?	1 2 3 4 5
3.	People with good character work better with others.	1 2 3 4 5
4.	Leaders cannot rise above the limitations of their character.	1 2 3 4 5

2. CHARISMA

5.	Do you love life?	1 2 3 4 5
6.	You expect that others can do well (you put a "10" on every person's head).	1 2 3 4 5
7.	Do you give people hope?	1 2 3 4 5
8.	Do you share your knowledge and time?	1 2 3 4 5
9.	Do you avoid taking work problems home?	1 2 3 4 5

3. COMMITMENT

10.	Are you really committed to your commitments?	1 2 3 4 5
11.	Do you demonstrate your commitment with actions?	1 2 3 4 5
12.	Do you strive to achieve your goals?	1 2 3 4 5

4. COMMUNICATION

13.	Do you communicate your message clearly?	1 2 3 4 5
14.	Do you truly see the other person when communicating?	1 2 3 4 5
15.	Do you always speak the truth?	1 2 3 4 5
16.	Do you actively seek responses from others?	1 2 3 4 5

5. COMPETENCE

17. Are you ready to be engaged every day?		1	2	3	4	5
18. Do you keep improving?		1	2	3	4	5
19. Do you follow through with excellence?		1	2	3	4	5
20. Are you accomplishing more than expected?		1	2	3	4	5
21. Do you inspire others?		1	2	3	4	5

6. COURAGE

22. Are you doing what you are afraid to do?		1	2	3	4	5
23. Do you stand up for your convictions?		1	2	3	4	5
24. Are you able to encourage others?		1	2	3	4	5
25. Do you inspire commitment within others?		1	2	3	4	5

7. DISCERNMENT

26. Do you discover root issues?		1	2	3	4	5
27. Are you improving your problem-solving skills?		1	2	3	4	5
28. Do you evaluate your options for maximum impact?		1	2	3	4	5
29. Do you strive to multiply your opportunities?		1	2	3	4	5

8. FOCUS

30. Are you focused on your strengths?		1	2	3	4	5
31. Are you focused on new opportunities?		1	2	3	4	5
32. Do you avoid focusing on weaknesses?		1	2	3	4	5

9. GENEROSITY

33. Are you grateful for whatever you have?		1	2	3	4	5
34. Are you putting people first?		1	2	3	4	5
35. Do you avoid letting possessions control you?		1	2	3	4	5
36. Do you regard money as a resource?		1	2	3	4	5
37. Are you developing the habit of giving?		1	2	3	4	5

10. INITIATIVE

38. Do you know what you want?	1	2	3	4	5
39. Do you push yourself to act?	1	2	3	4	5
40. Do you take more risks?	1	2	3	4	5
41. Do you learn from mistakes?	1	2	3	4	5

11. LISTENING

42. Do you spend time with all team members?	1	2	3	4	5
43. Do you spend time getting information about competitors?	1	2	3	4	5
44. Do you use a mentor?	1	2	3	4	5

12. PASSION

45. Do you show enthusiasm?	1	2	3	4	5
46. Do you want things as much as you want air?	1	2	3	4	5
47. Is your passion influencing your personality?	1	2	3	4	5
48. Do you believe you can make possible the impossible?	1	2	3	4	5

13. POSITIVE ATTITUDE

49. Do you understand that attitude is a choice?	1	2	3	4	5
50. Do you believe your attitude determines your actions?	1	2	3	4	5
51. Do you see a mirror of your attitude in other people?	1	2	3	4	5
52. Do you maintain a good attitude?	1	2	3	4	5

14. PROBLEM SOLVING

53. Do you anticipate problems?	1	2	3	4	5
54. Do you accept the truth?	1	2	3	4	5
55. Are you able to see the big picture?	1	2	3	4	5
56. Do you handle one thing at a time?	1	2	3	4	5
57. Do you still pursue major goals even when you are down?	1	2	3	4	5

15. RELATIONSHIPS

58. Do you understand people?	1 2 3 4 5
59. Do you help people?	1 2 3 4 5

16. RESPONSIBILITY

60. Do you get the job done?	1 2 3 4 5
61. Are you willing to go the extra mile?	1 2 3 4 5
62. Are you driven by excellence?	1 2 3 4 5
63. Are you productive regardless of the situation?	1 2 3 4 5

17. SECURITY

64. Do you provide security for others?	1 2 3 4 5
65. Do you give more to people than you take?	1 2 3 4 5
66. Do you avoid limiting your best people?	1 2 3 4 5
67. Do you avoid limiting the organization?	1 2 3 4 5

18. SELF-DISCIPLINE

68. Do you develop and follow your priorities?	1 2 3 4 5
69. Do you make a disciplined lifestyle your goal?	1 2 3 4 5
70. Do you get the job done instead of make excuses?	1 2 3 4 5
71. Do you limit rewards until the job is done?	1 2 3 4 5
72. Do you stay focused on results?	1 2 3 4 5

19. SERVANTHOOD

73. Are you putting others ahead of your own agenda?	1 2 3 4 5
74. Do you possess the confidence to serve?	1 2 3 4 5
75. Do you initiate service to others?	1 2 3 4 5
76. Do you regularly feel obliged to serve others?	1 2 3 4 5
77. Do you help others stay focused on results?	1 2 3 4 5
78. Do you love people?	1 2 3 4 5

20. TEACHABILITY

79. Do you think you can grow more?   1 2 3 4 5
80. Do you still keep working even after you succeed?   1 2 3 4 5
81. Are you determined to put in the effort to succeed?   1 2 3 4 5
82. Do you overcome the fear of making mistakes?   1 2 3 4 5
83. Do you avoid paying twice for the same mistake?   1 2 3 4 5

21. VISION

84. Do you have a personal vision?   1 2 3 4 5
85. Is your vision adding value to your team?   1 2 3 4 5
86. Is your vision meeting other's needs?   1 2 3 4 5
87. Is your vision helping you to gather resources?   1 2 3 4 5
88. Do you get others to share your vision?   1 2 3 4 5

How to calculate your score:

First, count the number of 1s that you circled and write that number next to 1x under CALCULATIONS. Do the same for all of the 2s, 3s, 4s, and 5s you circled.

Multiply the number you wrote down in each of the blanks by the number to the left (1, 2, 3, 4, or 5). Write each of these subtotals in the blanks to the right of the equals sign, then add them to get your total score.

CALCULATIONS

1 x _____ = _____

2 x _____ = _____

3 x _____ = _____

4 x _____ = _____

5 x _____ = _____

TOTAL SCORE _____

Are you a good leader?

Scoring	Meaning
0–88	Make a concerted effort to address all leadership characteristics. Study hard. Seek a mentor. Pay attention to how others address similar issues. If all seems hopeless, try something else.
89–176	You need focused work. Ask for feedback from others. Attend leadership training.
177–264	Your leadership skills are average, and there is room for improvement. Find ways to develop unique skills that enable you to stand out. Achieve small successes; learn from those successes and apply lessons learned to achieve greater successes.
265–352	You are almost there. Keep improving. Help others. Maintain a positive attitude.
353–440	Congratulations—you are almost complete. Be a mentor. Share your wisdom. Serve as an example for others to emulate.

The following toolset offers suggestions to help you improve your leadership skills in these 21 dimensions.

TOOLSET: CHECKLIST OF QUALITIES FOR 21ST CENTURY LEADERS

To be an effective leader, practice and develop all the following qualities and skills.

What To Do	How To Do It
Character	☐ Study all areas of your projects, and identify where you might have cut corners, compromised, or let people down. ☐ Look for patterns in your own behavior and others' that point toward either positive or negative traits. ☐ Face the music. Create a list of people to whom you need to apologize for your actions, then follow through with sincere apologies. ☐ Rebuild. Create a plan that prevents you from making the same mistakes again.
Charisma	☐ Love life—if you want to attract people, you need to be like the people you enjoy being with. ☐ Express high expectations for the people you work with—put a "10" on every person's head. ☐ Give people hope; be a dealer of hope. ☐ Share your wisdom, resources, and even special occasions with others.
Commitment	☐ Measure it. Sometimes we think we are committed to something, yet our actions indicate otherwise; measurement ensures consistency. ☐ Know what is "worth dying for." Take some time to contemplate what is really important. Do your actions match your ideals? ☐ Make your plans public. This may strengthen your commitment to follow through with them.
Communication	☐ Simplify your message, and keep it simple. ☐ Really see the person with whom you are communicating. ☐ Speak the truth. Credibility precedes great communication. ☐ Require responses from others. Do not forget that the goal of all communication is action.

Competence	☐ Show up every day ready to do your best. ☐ Keep improving. ☐ Consistently target excellence in performance. ☐ Accomplish more than expected. ☐ Inspire others through words, actions, and results.
Courage	☐ Courage begins with an inward battle. ☐ Courage is making things right, not just smoothing them over. ☐ Courage in a leader inspires commitment from followers. ☐ Push through your fears; expand into uncomfortable areas. Your life expands in proportion to your courage.
Discernment	☐ Discover the root issues behind problems. ☐ Enhance your problem-solving capacity. Try the TEACH process described below. ☐ Evaluate your options for maximum impact. ☐ Seek out opportunities. Realize how one opportunity may expand into multiple opportunities.
Focus	☐ Shift to your strengths. ☐ Staff your weaknesses. ☐ Create a strategy that offers a competitive advantage.
Generosity	☐ Give something away, such as time, money, goods, or services. ☐ Invest time, money, goods, or services. ☐ Find someone to mentor.
Initiative	☐ Be a proactive instigator. ☐ Don't wait for opportunity to knock. ☐ Take the next step.
Listening	☐ Allow time in your schedule to really listen to your followers, competitors, customers, and mentors. ☐ Meet people on their turf; ask them about themselves. ☐ Listen between the lines. Do not ignore the emotional content of the conversation.

Passion	☐ Take your "temperature"—evaluate how you really feel about the work you are doing.
	☐ Return to your first love.
	☐ Associate with people who are passionate.
Positive attitude	☐ Feed yourself daily by taking in positive messages and surrounding yourself with positive people.
	☐ Achieve a goal every day.
	☐ Remind yourself of your purpose and beliefs through daily affirmations.
Problem-solving	☐ Develop a method to identify and solve problems. Try the TEACH process: – Time: spend time to discover the real issue – Exposure: find out what others have done – Assistance: have your team study all angles – Creativity: brainstorm multiple solutions – Hit it: implement the best solution.
	☐ Surround yourself with problem solvers.
Relationships	☐ Improve your mind through readings, studies, and discussions.
	☐ Strengthen your heart—practice empathy and pay attention to feelings.
	☐ Repair hurt relationships.
Responsibility	☐ Keep hanging in there.
	☐ Admit it when your efforts are not good enough.
	☐ Find better tools.
Security	☐ Know your strengths and vulnerabilities.
	☐ Give credit where credit is due.
	☐ Help others expand rather than remain limited.
Self-discipline	☐ Sort out your priorities.
	☐ Know and share reasons for your actions.
	☐ Get rid of excuses.

Servanthood	☐ Perform small acts.
	☐ Learn to walk slowly through the crowd—don't rush through your interactions with other people.
	☐ Take action to improve what others experience due to your actions.
Teachability	☐ Observe how you react to mistakes.
	☐ Try something new.
	☐ Operate in your areas of strength.
Vision	☐ Assess what matters to you, and what is realistically achievable.
	☐ Do a gut check—what activities inspire you or make you ill?
	☐ Answer the following questions: What makes you cry? What do you dream about? What gives you energy or inspires you?
	☐ Based on your answers to the questions above, formulate and write down your personal, project, and organizational visions.
	☐ Validate with others that your vision is clear, concise, convincing, and compelling.

TOOLSET: ATTITUDE IS EVERYTHING

Human beings are like sponges: we soak up whatever those around us are saying. Unfortunately, we can't always distinguish between messages that are good for us and those that aren't. If you hear something often enough, you tend to believe it and act on it.

That's why negative colleagues can be so harmful. They try to drag you down to their level. They hammer away at you by harping on all the things that you supposedly can't do, things they say are impossible. These people can be called "dream killers" or "energy vampires," because they suck all the positive energy out of you. Eventually, you get frustrated and lose motivation.

Compare that with how you feel when you're around team members who are enthusiastic and supportive. You pick up their attitude and you feel as if you have gained more strength to vigorously pursue your own goals. You're energized and inspired—and you perform better.

The people who occupy your time have a significant impact on your most priceless possession: your mind. Now and then, it is important to assess your relationships with colleagues—even those you've worked with for many years. Are you surrounding yourself with negative people? If so, consider spending much less time (or no time at all) with them.

Of course, you can't always choose who you work with. Many times you have to cope with negative colleagues; you may not have the option to avoid them. In those cases, follow these practices:

- **Discover the roots of their negativity.** Perhaps they don't feel appreciated or they didn't feel supported on earlier projects. Understanding is the first step.

- **Remind them every day that they have a choice.** They may not be able to change the project or organizational situations, but they can choose to be happy (or unhappy).

- **Ask them to make an effort to be more positive.** That includes curbing their use of words such as *failure* and *impossible*.

- **Show them you care.** Speak to all team members for at least a few minutes every day, and they will soon understand that you care about them. Concerned, loving, respectful leaders can move mountains.

Such actions can help get at the root cause of your colleagues' negativity and begin to turn them into positive people. As you increase your associations with positive people, you will feel better about yourself and will have renewed force to achieve your goals. You will become a more upbeat person—the kind of person others love to be around— and your work will reflect that.

We used to think it was merely helpful to associate with positive people and to limit involvement with negative people. Now we believe it is absolutely *essential*. Surround yourself with positive people, and they will lift you up the ladder of success.

TOOLSET: PROJECT MANAGER TEACHABILITY

Here are guidelines to help cultivate and maintain a teachable attitude:

- **Cure your "destination disease."** Lack of teachability is often rooted in achievement. Some project managers mistakenly believe that if they can accomplish a particular goal, they no longer have to grow. Complete project managers cannot afford to think that way. The day they stop growing is the day they forfeit their potential and the potential of the organization.

- **Overcome your success.** Effective project leaders know that what got them to a particular level does not keep them there. If you have been a successful project manager in the past, beware. Consider this: if what you did yesterday still looks big to you, you have not done much today.

- **Swear off shortcuts.** If you want to grow as a project manager in a particular area, figure out what it will really take, including the price, and then determine to pay it.

- **Trade in your pride.** Teachability requires us to admit we do not know everything, and that can make us look bad. One of the greatest mistakes one can make as a project manager is to continually fear you will make one.

- **Never pay twice for the same mistake.** Whoever makes no mistakes makes no progress. But the leader who keeps making the same mistakes also makes no progress. For every mistake you make, focus on what it taught you.

In order to improve your teachability, do the following:

- **Observe how you react to your mistakes.** Do you admit your mistakes? Do you apologize when appropriate, or are you defensive? Observe yourself. You are a project leader, and your team expects you to lead by example. If you react badly or you make no mistakes at all, you need to work on your teachability.

- **Try something new.** Get out of your project rut today and do something different that will stretch you mentally, emotionally, or physically. Challenges change us for the better. If you really want to start growing, make new challenges part of everyday activities.

- **Learn in your area of strength.** Read 6 to 12 books a year on leadership or on project management. Continuing to learn in an area where you are already an expert prevents you from becoming jaded and unteachable. Becoming an expert (in anything) requires 10,000 hours of study, according to leadership authors Kouzes and Posner (2007).

TOOLSET: LISTENING TO PEOPLE

We have observed these listening behaviors:

- **Hearing:** The listener hears your comments but does not process anything in his brain. He then forgets the message.

- **Information gathering:** She is just collecting information, not really listening to anything other than the specific information she is seeking.

- **Cynical listening:** He seems to be listening to you and is nodding along as you speak—but these are deceptive behaviors because he is thinking about something else, not actually listening.

- **Offensive listening:** She is not focused on you as you talk. She does not look at you or is doing other things while listening—perhaps working on a computer or answering a call.

- **Polite listening:** His listening manners are good—he is quiet and looks at you as you speak—but how much is he really absorbing?

- **Active listening:** She paraphrases and validates what she understood about your talk.

Listening is hard work. Unlike hearing, listening demands total concentration. Listening is an active search for meaning, while hearing is passive. Try to listen with these questions in mind:

- What is the speaker saying?
- What does it mean?
- How does it relate to what was said before?
- What point is the speaker trying to make?
- How can I use the information the speaker is giving me?
- Does it make sense?
- Am I getting the whole story?
- Is the speaker supporting his or her points?
- How does this relate to what I already know?

Also ask questions, especially clarifying questions. Words have definitions, but meaning comes from the person who is speaking. To understand the full meaning, you may have to help the speaker by following up with questions. Maintaining eye contact and nodding occasionally, when appropriate, also help to let the speaker know you are listening.

Paraphrase when you want to make sure you have understood, when you are not sure you have caught the meaning, and before you agree or disagree. Paraphrasing is also useful when dealing with people who repeat themselves—it assures them they have communicated their ideas to you.

Be cognizant of three levels in cross-cultural exchanges:

1. *Pay attention* to the person, his culture, his background, and the message.
2. *Create rapport* by finding some values in common.
3. *Share meaning*. Verbalize stereotypes and work through them to check that your understanding and the other person's are correct.

Listen better to project stakeholders, and you will learn more about your project.

TOOLSET: HOW ARE YOU LISTENING?

Every 30 days, score yourself on a scale from 1 to 10 (10 = maximum) in the following areas. Convert your score to a percentage (100 = 100%). Then record your results on the next pages to monitor your progress.

Questions	In a normal situation	Under stress
1. How much attention do you pay to the words the other person is saying to you when you are listening to him/her?		
2. How much attention do you pay to the tone of voice of the person who is talking to you?		
3. Do you wait to talk until the other person finishes?		
4. Do you maintain visual contact while talking?		
5. How well do you understand the other person's body language?		
6. When the other person is talking, do you listen fully, not partially? Do you focus on him/her rather than thinking about what you will say when he/she finishes talking?		
7. Do you always paraphrase the other person's words?		
8. Do you try to put yourself in the shoes of the speaker when listening?		
9. Do you apply different listening filters depending on the culture or gender of the speaker, such as how they view time, relationships, or conversations?		
10. Do you demonstrate interest in the other person when listening?		
Scoring	%	%

How was your scoring?

90–100%: Phenomenal

80–90%: Very good

70–80%: Good

60–70%: Medium

50–60%: You need to improve

40–50%: You need to improve a lot

SCORING RECORDS

Question	INITIAL		MONTH 1		MONTH 2		MONTH 3	
	Normal	Stress	Normal	Stress	Normal	Stress	Normal	Stress
1								
2								
3								
4								
5								
6								
7								
8								
9								
10								

	INITIAL		MONTH 4		MONTH 5		MONTH 6	
Question	Normal	Stress	Normal	Stress	Normal	Stress	Normal	Stress
1								
2								
3								
4								
5								
6								
7								
8								
9								
10								

TOOLSET: LISTENING IMPROVEMENT TOOL

For all the following skills, please write specific actions that you can take in order to improve. Pay particular attention to those areas in which your scores were lower.

Key areas for improvement	What will I do to improve?
Being present and communicating my interest in what the other person is saying	
Waiting until the other person finishes before starting to talk	
Listening completely and patiently before planning a response	
Listening to specific words versus global meaning	
Tone of voice/inflection	
Reading body language	
Repeating what I heard to confirm my understanding with the sender	
Empathy: being in the speaker's shoes	
Understanding how cultural, gender, and local differences affect communication	
Looking at the eyes of the other person when he or she is talking	
Using body language such as gestures to listen better	

TOOLSET: DEVELOPING RELATIONSHIPS UP THE ORGANIZATION

Here are some practices that we find extremely helpful in running projects within organizations:

Listen to your leader's heartbeat.

Try to understand what makes him or her tick. That may mean paying attention in informal settings, such as during hallway conversations, at lunch, or in the meeting that often occurs informally before or after a meeting. If you know your leader well and feel the relationship is solid, you may be more direct and ask questions about what really matters to him or her on an emotional level.

If you are not sure what to look for, focus on these three areas: What makes him laugh? This is very important. What makes him cry? This is what touches a person's heart at a deep emotional level. What makes him sing? These are the things that bring deep fulfillment.

All people have dreams, issues, or causes with which they connect deeply. Those things are like the keys to their lives. Are you aware of the things that touch *you* on a deep emotional level? What are the signs that they "connect" for you? Do you see those signs in your leader? Look for them, and you will likely find them.

Know your leader's priorities.

Leaders' priorities are the things they have to do. But priorities are more than just tasks on a to-do list. All leaders have duties that they must complete or they will fail in fulfilling their responsibilities. Priorities are those short-list responsibilities that your leader's boss would say are do-or-die for that position. Make it your goal to learn what those priorities are. The better acquainted you are with those duties or objectives, the better you will understand and communicate with your leader.

Catch your leader's enthusiasm.

It is much easier to work with someone when you share enthusiasm. If you can catch your leader's enthusiasm, it will have a similarly energizing effect on you, it will create a bond between you and your leader, and you will pass it on, because you will not be able to contain it.

Support your leader's vision.

When top leaders hear others articulate the vision they have cast for the organization, their hearts sing. This feeling is very rewarding. It represents a kind of *tipping point*, to use the words of author Malcolm Gladwell. It indicates a level of ownership by others in the organization that bodes well for the fulfillment of the vision. Leaders in the middle of the organization who are champions for the vision become elevated in the estimation of a top leader. They get it. They are on board. And they have great value to the organization.

Never underestimate the power of a verbal endorsement of a vision by a person with influence. As a leader in the middle, if you are unsure about the vision of your leader, then talk to that person. Ask questions. Once you think you understand it, quote it back to your leader (when appropriate) to make sure you are in alignment. If you got it right, you will be able to see it in your leader's face. Then start passing the vision on to the people in your sphere of influence. It will be good for the organization, your people, your leader, and you. Promote your leader's dreams, and that leader will promote you.

Connect with your leader's interests.

One of the keys to building relational chemistry is knowing and connecting with your leader's interests. It is important to know enough about your leader to be able to relate to him as an individual beyond the job. If your boss is a golfer, you may want to take up the game or at least learn some things about it. If he collects rare books or porcelain, then spend some time on the Internet finding out about these hobbies. Just learn enough to relate to your boss and talk intelligently about the subject.

Understand your leader's personality.

Two staff members were discussing the president of their company, and one of them said, "You know, you cannot help liking the guy." The other replied, "Yes, if you do not, he fires you." Leaders are used to having others accommodate their personalities. As you lead down from the middle of the organization, do you not expect others to conform to your personality? We do not mean, of course, that you should fire someone who does not like you. Your expectations should not be unreasonable, nor should you behave in a spiteful way toward people who do not conform to your preferences. But if you are simply being yourself, you expect the people who work for you to work with you. When you are trying to lead up, you are the one who needs to conform to your leader's personality. It is a rare great leader who conforms down to the people who work for him or her.

It is wise to understand your leader's style and how your personality styles interact. Most of the time, personality opposites get along well as long as their values and goals are similar. According to the temperament theory of the ancient Greeks, *cholerics* (doers) work well with *phlegmatics* (people who are self-content and kind); *sanguines* (extroverts) and *melancholics* (ponderers) appreciate each other's strengths. Trouble can come when people with similar personality types come together. If you find that your personality is similar to your boss's, then remember that you are the one who has to be flexible. That can be a challenge if yours is not a flexible personality type.

Earn your leader's trust.

When you take time to invest in relational chemistry with your leader, the eventual result will be trust—in other words, relational currency. When you do things that add to the relationship, you increase the amount of relational change in your pocket. When you do negative things, you spend that change. If you keep dropping the ball, professionally or personally, you harm the relationship, and you may eventually spend all of your relational currency and bankrupt the relationship.

Learn to work with your leader's weaknesses.

You cannot build a positive relationship with your boss if you secretly disrespect him because of his weaknesses. Since everybody has blind spots and weak areas, why not learn to work with them? Try to focus on the positives and work around the negatives. Doing anything else will only hurt you.

People can usually trace their successes and failures to the relationships in their lives. The same is true when it comes to leadership. The quality of the relationship you have with your leader will impact your success or failure. That investment is most worthwhile.

TOOLSET: GETTING EXTRAORDINARY PERFORMANCE

In a *Fast Company* article, "How to Lead Now," John A. Byrne (2003) summarizes ways to get extraordinary performance, especially when you can't pay for it.

- Studies of high-performing organizations show that eliciting great performance comes down to one core issue: building pride.

- Getting more productivity out of people comes not by cutting and slashing, but by nurturing, engaging, and recognizing.

- Researchers found that spending 10 percent of revenue on capital improvements boosts productivity by 3.9 percent, but a similar investment in developing human capital increases productivity by 8.5 percent—more than twice as much.

- "Money attracts and retains people better than it motivates them to excel."

- The push for pride-building comes from individuals within organizations—not from organizations themselves.

- Employees are no longer loyal to organizations as much as they are loyal to people.

- Pride-building is a task for front-line leaders who are closest to the real work of a corporation.

- Commitment and loyalty derive solely from the relationships that leaders develop with the people who report to them.

- Personalize the workplace, cultivating close-knit communities inside large, often impersonal corporations.

- Pride, happiness, and feeling good come from being part of a winning team.

- It is possible to create a group of people who will do anything in the world for a leader.

- Create self-reinforcing peer groups of four to seven senior people across the company, connect them via email and phone calls, and have them compete with other teams.

- Assign mentoring roles to veterans to assist younger staffers.

- Set goals to re-create people's pride in their work, team, and organization.

- Focus on creating engagement that makes a difference.

- Remember that work is indeed personal, as it always has been.

- Jon R. Katzenbach describes an effective pride-building process in *Why Pride Matters More Than Money* (2003):
  - Personalize the workplace.
  - Always have your compass set on pride, not money.
  - Localize as much as possible.
  - Make your messages simple and direct.

TOOLSET: MANAGING YOUR EXECUTIVES

Michael O'Brochta, PMP, president of Zozer Inc. in Roanoke, Virginia, shared his action steps for influencing executives in a paper, "How to Accelerate Executive Support for Projects" (2011):

> Project managers are falling into the trap of applying best-practice project management only to have the project fail because of executive inaction or counteraction. Project managers who continue doing what used to work by focusing within the bounds of the project are now finding success more difficult to achieve. The problem is that project success is dependent, to an increasing degree, not only on the efforts of the project manager but also on the efforts of the executive.
>
> The topic of accelerating executive support for projects falls within the broader context of project success. If we visualize this context as a process, we can focus on examining the actual criteria for project success in the process, and then we can examine the actions we can take as project managers to ensure the project is successful. An expanded definition of success now includes factors well beyond the control or influence of the project manager; executive actions for project success must also be taken to support the efforts of the project manager. This consideration now takes the topic of project success to a whole new level. This new level, which goes well beyond traditional project management, involves great project management and involves focusing outside the traditional bounds of the project, focusing on the executive, and focusing on getting the executive to act for project success.
>
> A challenge is to get executives to overcome barriers—such as the demands of their executive responsibilities, the constraints they encounter (both real and imagined), and their limited understanding of the discipline of project management—and actually take action to support projects. At this point, the project manager can adopt a range of attitudes regarding his or her involvement. This attitude range can be characterized as a continuum between passive and active.
>
> At the passive end of the continuum [see Figure 1-1], the project manager remains focused internally on the project, using traditional project management techniques, and pays relatively little attention to changing the workplace environment to enable better project success. Here, we have the project manager accepting the status quo and largely detaching him- or herself from efforts to help the executive overcome the barriers and act for project success.
>
> At the active end of the continuum, the project manager accepts broad responsibility for success of the project and engages in efforts to reshape

the workplace environment to support the needs of the project. Here, we have the project manager actively engaged in a codependent relationship with the executive, a relationship in which both parties understand that their success is dependent on each other. Here, we have the project manager expanding his or her focus beyond the traditional project bounds to include helping the executive overcome the barriers and act for project success.

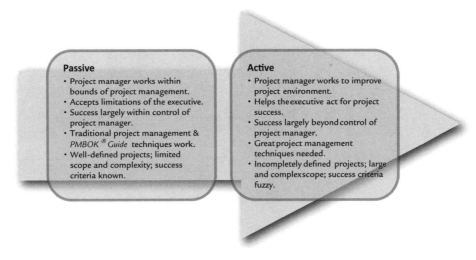

Passive
- Project manager works within bounds of project management.
- Accepts limitations of the executive.
- Success largely within control of project manager.
- Traditional project management & *PMBOK® Guide* techniques work.
- Well-defined projects; limited scope and complexity; success criteria known.

Active
- Project manager works to improve project environment.
- Helps the executive act for project success.
- Success largely beyond control of project manager.
- Great project management techniques needed.
- Incompletely defined projects; large and complex scope; success criteria fuzzy.

FIGURE 1-1:   Shifting Behaviors to Win Greater Executive Support

Executive Support for Projects Model

I developed a new two-dimensional model (see Figure 1-2) to gauge the level of executive support for projects. This model includes scales for accessing the **attitude** of the executive as well as the **ability** of the executive. I then provide guidance for how to use the model to guide action. The Executive Support for Projects Model is intended as an aid in assessing and diagnosing the organizational environment in which the project manager and executive reside. Armed with a level of understanding about the nature of an executive's support for projects, the project manager is more likely to find an effective approach to help the executive take the actions for project success. Note that the model represents *observable behavior* of the executive and can be used to assist in determining the underlying reasons for the behavior.

The Executive Attitude axis is a continuum that represents the attitude of the executive toward taking actions for project success. At the high end of the scale, executives are characterized as proactive—taking initiative to identify and act on opportunities that they see as supportive of project success. The midpoint on the scale pertains to executives who are reactive—those who take supportive action in response to a stimulus from the situation or project manager. The low end of the scale represents behavior that is counter to the goal of acting for project success; actions taken at this end of the scale reduce the likelihood of project success.

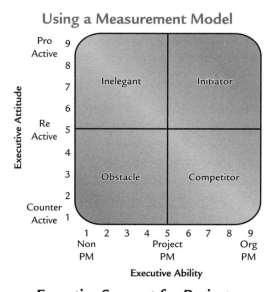

Executive Support for Projects

FIGURE 1-2:   Executive Measurement Model

The Executive Ability axis is a continuous range representing the project management–related ability of the executive. At the high end of the scale, executives are characterized as being adept at not only the management of projects but also at the management of the organization in which the project resides; organizational change is a skill possessed by these executives. The midpoint on the scale pertains to executives who have a full set of skills to manage within the bounds of a defined project but who are not equipped to impact the organizational environment in which the project is located. The low end of the scale represents executives who, although they may possess a significant range of skills, are not able to manage projects or impact the project environment.

By using the Executive Support for Projects Model, the project manager can gauge both the executive's attitude and ability. Taken together, these two dimensions serve as the basis of understanding needed to allow the project manager to help the executive overcome the barriers and accelerate support for project success. The resulting executive supports for project behaviors are as follows:

	Executive Behavior	Project Manager Acceleration Approach
Initiator	Proactive attitude and organizational project management ability. Concern for taking actions for project success. Thorough knowledge of the management of projects within the organizational context. High motivation to use foresight to identify upcoming opportunities.	Full and open communications with executive to ensure that actions for project success are synchronized.
Inelegant	Proactive attitude and non–project management ability. Concern for taking action for project success, but without the benefit of needed understanding about project management. Likelihood of well-intentioned actions being taken that are less than effective.	Take the lead to identify the actions for the executive to take and help executive take those actions.
Competitor	Counteractive attitude and organizational project management ability. Agendas counter to project success. Thorough knowledge of the management of projects within the organizational context. Likely to subjugate project management to achieve competing agenda.	Keep well informed of the executive's actions and look for common ground to reduce the level of competition.
Obstacle	Counteractive attitude and non–project management ability. Concern for agendas counter to project success, but without the benefit of the understanding needed for project management. Likelihood of somewhat random and unpredictable behavior that may or may not impact project success.	Insulate the executive, form alliance with a more supportive executive, and raise the opposing executive's project management knowledge level.

THE ROLE OF HUMOR AND FUN

TOOLSET: USING HUMOR

The project manager is obligated to have a plan and make project activities happen. Usually the plan does not reflect what is going to happen but what you want to happen. Changes are inevitable, so you as a project manager need to prioritize and manage time well. Timothy C. shares this story as told by a supervisor to his superiors when asked why his employees were so successful and motivated yet always seemed to be laughing and chatting:

> A teacher is giving a lecture. On his desk is a bag of sand, a bag of pebbles, some big rocks, and a bucket. The teacher places the big rocks in the bucket, filling it to the top. He then asks his students if the bucket is full, to which his students reply, "Yes, the bucket is full." The teacher then takes the pebbles and pours them on top of the larger rocks while shaking the bucket, filling the gaps between the larger rocks. Again the teacher asks his students if the bucket is full, to which his students reply yes. The teacher then takes the bag of sand and pours it in the bucket, filling in the gaps left between the larger and smaller rocks. Again the teacher asks his students if the bucket is full. To which his students reply, "Yes, without a doubt, the bucket is indeed full." The teacher then reaches under his desk and produces a beer. He opens it up and pours it into the bucket, completely filling the bucket.
>
> The teacher then tells his students that the large rocks symbolize the large tasks in your life, the pebbles the medium tasks, and the sand the small tasks. Only by tackling the large tasks first, followed by the medium, and finally the small tasks can things be accomplished.
>
> "But sir," says one student, slouched at the back of the classroom, "You've forgotten one thing…the beer."
>
> To which the teacher replies, "The beer symbolizes that no matter how busy you are, there's always time for a beer."

This humorous story was all the explanation Timothy's manager needed to give to explain why his employees were successful and motivated: they completed the biggest tasks first and celebrated their success at the end.

A version of this story that we found on the web has another twist: a volunteer was solicited to put the items in the jar. The volunteer started with the sand, then the pebbles, followed by the large rocks, which did not fit. Reversing the order leads to another point, which Stephen R. Covey, A. Roger Merrill, and Rebecca R. Merrill describe in their book, *First Things First* (1994). The big idea is that you must schedule time for your most important priorities *first*. If you do not, you will never get to them. A corollary to this principle is this: *what gets scheduled gets done.* The opposite is also true: *what doesn't get scheduled doesn't get done.*

What are your "big rocks" that you need to schedule first? If you are not careful to do so, the tyranny of the *urgent* will crowd out the *important,* as Covey says.

One way for project managers to think of this example is to see the rocks as project scheduled tasks. The pebbles are requests for changes that need to be analyzed and take time. The sand represents interpersonal and political conflicts that weave their way throughout all activities and need to be managed on a daily basis. Of course, the beer is a reminder to take breaks and have fun.

Team-building exercises are more effective if you include opportunities for people to laugh and have fun. When starting work with a new team, we put together a team "bonding session." The goal of the exercise was for the team members to get acquainted by answering a few questions set forth by the project manager:

- What are your professional strengths?
- What are your professional weaknesses?
- What are you hobbies?
- Are you married/single?
- Do you have kids?
- Are there any skeletons in your closet?

For most of the questions team members were quite serious when describing themselves or their situation, but when it came to talking about the skeletons in their closets, the team really started laughing and enjoying their time together. It ended up being a good exercise: team members got to know each other better and shared laughs, which really opened up new discussions.

TOOLSET: HOW TO USE LAUGHTER

Laughter is one of our all-time favorite stress management strategies because it is free, convenient, and beneficial in so many ways. Try some of the following strategies to bring more laughter into your life:

- **TV and movies:** There is no shortage of funny movies, TV shows, and online videos. While wasting time watching something marginally funny may actually be frustrating rather than relaxing, watching truly hilarious movies and shows is an easy way to bring laughter into your life whenever it is needed. Show video clips at team meetings to break from routine and stimulate different thinking.

- **Laugh with friends:** Going to a movie or comedy club with friends is a great way to laugh together. The contagious effects of laughter may mean people laugh more than they otherwise would have during the show, plus they have jokes to reference later. Having friends over for a party or game night is also a great setup for laughter and other good feelings. Gather team members at off-site locations to have fun together.

- **Find humor in your project:** Instead of complaining about the frustrations on your project, try to laugh about them. If something is so frustrating or depressing it is ridiculous, realize that you just might look back on it and laugh. Imagine telling your friends the story of the project, then see if you can laugh about it now. With this attitude, you may also find yourself being more lighthearted and silly, giving yourself and those around you more to laugh about. Approach projects in a more mirthful way, and you will find you are less stressed about negative events—and you will achieve the health benefits of laughter at the same time. Also, try faking it until you make it—just as studies show that people gain the positive effects of smiling whether the smile is fake or real, faked laughter also provides the benefits mentioned above. So smile more and fake laughter; you will still achieve positive effects, and the fake merriment may lead to real smiles and laughter.

- **More on having fun:** See additional suggestions in *The Complete Project Manager* on laughing more and having fun in your projects and in your life. Leverage examples from others about practices, fun activities, and jokes that work well for them.

TOOLSET: APPLYING HUMOR

We first heard this joke after dinner at an international project management conference in Oslo, Norway.

The German president of the association introduced a British consultant who shared a few words of humor.

"In heaven we will find a French cook, a German engineer, an English policeman, and an Italian lover. If we are unlucky enough to go to hell, we will find a French engineer, a German lover, an English cook, and an Italian policeman."

The joke was appropriate because it reflected the international makeup of the audience, and it made a friendly, teasing reference to the officers of the association and the countries they came from. It drew upon stereotypes to make its point but in a positive manner. It caused people to think about dominant characteristics of people and revel in the differences.

No one was harmed or offended by this joke, and its telling was timely and memorable.

Projector Humor

No matter how prepared you are for your presentation, there's a chance that something will not go smoothly. For those times when you've got a burned-out projector bulb, the extension cord won't reach, or you can't get an image to appear on the screen, break the ice (and embarrassing silence) with some humor.

Bulb issues:

"Does anybody happen to have a [*long description, recited quickly*] quartz two-prong, 921 EYB, 25-volt, 250-watt overhead projector lamp on them?"

"These overheads/slides are a little darker than I expected."

"Don't worry. We'll pass out blankets, pillows, and warm milk in a minute."

"I do my best work in the dark."

[*Pretend to find a service tag and read it*] "Last serviced by Thomas Edison…"

"I know what you're thinking: 'How many speakers does it take to change a light bulb?'"

General malfunctions:

[*Turn to the projector and pat it nicely.*] "Sunshine, have I told you how lovely you look? Now how 'bout you show us those slides?"

[*In an overly enthusiastic voice*] "Join hands, everyone. We're gonna sing campfire songs."

"That's all right. Lincoln didn't need one of these to deliver the Gettysburg Address, right?"

[*Walking off*] "We'll be RIGHT back after this message from our sponsor..."

"Well, that concludes today's presentation. Any questions?"

Garbled text:

"Does anyone speak gibberish?"

"I knew it. The projector's been taken over by ALIENS!"

No image:

[*Make shadow animals with your hands*] "Welcome to Shadow Puppet Theater!"

[*Wave a hand in front of the lens*] "Wake up in there. YOO-HOO. Anybody home?" ("Projector Humor" n.d.)

Lou Russell of Russell Martin and Associates shared some fun thoughts for addressing on-the-job burnout with humor (2003):

> Remember the five simple rules to be happy: 1. Free your heart from hatred. 2. Free your mind from worries. 3. Live simply. 4. Give more. 5. Expect less.
>
> And a little fantasy to help you deal with your burnout temporarily, here are some things you'd love to say at work....
> - I don't know what your problem is, but I'll bet it's hard to pronounce.
> - I'll try being nicer if you'll try being smarter.
> - You are validating my inherent mistrust of strangers.
> - Thank you. We're all refreshed and challenged by your unique point of view.
> - Any connection between your reality and mine is purely coincidental.
> - Do I look like a people person?
> - Sarcasm...just one more service we offer. (2003)

TOOLSET: YOUR SENSE OF HUMOR

In spotlighting "soft skills for hard times," Jim Czegledi (2011) shares these suggestions:

> Seeing things through a lens of humour opens you to being positive and to creative possibilities [and helps you] actively cultivate an ability to see that the glass is half full and think of options first rather than limits. For example, when humourous and positive project managers see a glass half full, they think that they have twice as much glass as necessary!
>
> Humour can help bridge any communication gaps and get everyone on the same page. It is oil that lubricates your relationships with others, reducing interpersonal frictions and keeping relationships running smoothly. When I feel that it is appropriate to lighten the mood of a conversation and I am asked where do I live? I say that I live very near where I was born and raised. I go on to say, that all those people who said that I wouldn't get very far in life, were right! This example of a little levity can go a long way to quickly establishing a relationship through the rapport of healthy humour. It is also glue that bonds people together and to the task you have set before them. It can help relax and energize your team building enabling them to do the work that needs to be done.

Seven Habits of Pretty Mirthful People (PMPs)

PMPs:
- Laugh with people, not at them;
- Are not rude, crude or lewd;
- Bond people together without putting anyone down;
- Poke gentle fun at what they sometimes do;
- Take what others do seriously and themselves lightly;
- Stay open to new thinking, relationships and possibilities; and
- [Try] to see the lighter side of life.

TOOLSET: PROJECT MANAGEMENT HUMOR

José Pinto, founder, director, and current president of the PMI®—Portugal Chapter, shares some humorous truths about project management in an issue of the Organizational Project Management Community of Practice email newsletter (2011):

1. Any task, no matter how complex, can be estimated accurately, once it's completed.

2. The most valuable, and least used, word in a project manager's vocabulary is "no."

3. Nothing is impossible for the person who doesn't have to do it.

4. You can bully a project manager into committing to an impossible project completion date, but you cannot bully him into meeting it.

5. Too few people on a project can't solve the problems—too many create more problems than they solve.

6. A change freeze is like the abominable snowman: it is a myth and would anyway melt when heat is applied.

7. A user will tell you anything you ask about, but nothing more.

8. A user is somebody who tells you what they really want the day you give them what they first asked for.

9. The conditions attached to a promise are forgotten; only the promise is remembered.

10. There's never enough time to do it right first time, but there's always enough time to go back and do it again.

11. I know that you believe that you understand what you think I said, but I am not sure you realize that what you heard is not what I meant.

12. The sooner you rush into coding, the later you finish the project.

13. If project scope is allowed to change freely, the rate of change will exceed the rate of progress.

14. Change is inevitable, except from vending machines.

15. The person who says it will take the longest and cost the most is the only one with a clue how to do the job.

16. The bitterness of poor product quality lingers long after the celebration of meeting the project date is forgotten.

17. A verbal contract isn't worth the paper it's written on.

18. What has not been put on paper has not been said.

19. If you fail to plan the project, you are planning to fail the project.

20. The more you plan the project, the luckier you get.

21. If you can keep your head while all about you are losing theirs, you haven't understood the project plan.

22. If you don't attack the project risks, the project risks will attack you.

23. A little bit of project risk management saves a lot of fan cleaning.

24. The sooner you fall behind the project schedule, the more time you have to make it up.

25. When all is said and done, a lot more was said then was done.

TOOLSET: DEMONSTRATING CONCEPTS USING HUMOR

In my (Englund) experience with professional organizations sponsoring major events, an inordinate amount of discussion goes into pessimistic forecasting and angst around break-even points. After suffering through these discussions quietly for a while, it becomes apparent that actions and thoughts are guided from an individual or self-serving frame of reference. We say this is operating in my own circle, separated from others, and feeling frustrated, almost paralyzed from acting. I'm doing my job, just leave me alone. I know what's best.

A new perspective is possible: operating in a different circle or frame of reference, where I connect with others in order to achieve a greater outcome. That means I speak up and remind the group of the "First Law of Money": money will come when you are doing the right thing. I refocus the discussion on why we are doing the event, reinforce that its purpose is to contribute to the professional community (not just prevent the organization from losing money), and engage others in clarifying the value the event offers, both to promoters and participants. If the value is indeed there, we can charge appropriately for the event, and people will come. We need to be enthusiastic about the project. It is that enthusiasm, and its source, that will be contagious, bringing others in to participate and making the project successful. I have shifted from managing myself to leading for results, where it becomes necessary to interact with other people.

This example highlights the two circles—individual and connected—that represent a revised way of thinking (see Figure 2-1).

One way to teach or demonstrate concepts such as the two circles is via humorous stories or video clips. In the movie *The Money Pit*, Tom Hanks's character buys a house that looks good at first, but he and his wife discover it needs lots of work. When fixing a stairway, he slams his finger with the hammer—and the whole stairway collapses. Later, he slips into a hole in the floor while holding his money. We laugh at the physical comedy, but we can learn from this. By trying to do all the work himself, Tom is operating in an individual circle. Then a motley cast of characters is summoned to do the fix-up work, and by the end of the movie the house looks marvelous. This happens because a connected circle is in operation.

The trick is to be aware in the moment of which frame is driving current thoughts and actions. Perhaps the other frame would be a more effective and appropriate approach. For example, I may be fixated on completing a management report that is required for an upcoming checkpoint meeting (individual circle). I forget to solicit inputs and review of the report by the client or team members (connected circle). It may have been expedient to make this decision on my own rather than engaging others, but failing to include others may create morale or trust issues that

will have a negative impact on the outcome of the project that is much more significant than the positive impact of fulfilling the output task by completing the report.

Resetting my thinking may drive me to take the time and effort to get inputs
from other stakeholders, realizing that I gain more respect and cooperation when
functioning in a collaborative mode. And the report may improve dramatically when
others point out errors, omissions, or new ideas. (Speaking of reports, one funny
way to determine if anyone reads it is to insert a joke line somewhere in the middle,
something like "This page will be copied from the Santa Clara phone directory."
Hopefully, readers will chuckle. When I [Englund] did this, just one person mentioned it to me. That told me she had read the report—but made me question if
anybody else did...).

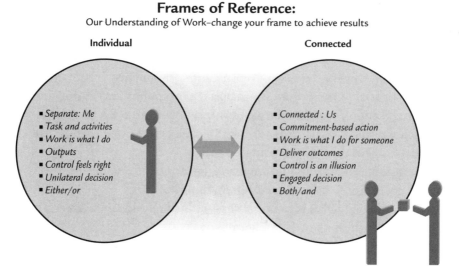

FIGURE 2-1:   Two-Circle Frames of Reference

An opposite example can emerge in the connected circle: if "groupthink" takes over
and people stop thinking on their own. If this happens, an individual may need to
shift to the individual circle and become a maverick. Humorous references to "lem-
mings marching to the sea"—following a leader to their destruction—can help people understand what is going on.

In short, you can use humor, such as a funny example or video clip, to demonstrate the two basic frames of reference and make people aware of which circle they
are operating in at any moment. The next step is to ask if what they or you are doing
is the best way to handle the situation. You and they then have the option to switch
circles and act differently. The point is not to determine which circle is "better"
overall but to decide which frame of reference is best for the situation.

PERSONAL SKILLS

TOOLSET: CONVERSATION AS A PROJECT RESOURCE

High-performance cultures require leaders who leverage their self-awareness, understand their leadership style, and place value on the power of strong relationships. These leaders are fully aware that sustaining effort and achieving project results are a function of interaction and interdependence. They know that developing strong working relationships is one of the keys to sustained success.

Complete project managers increase their awareness of how important conversation is to project communication and organizational learning. They develop specific techniques and values for team members to use conversations effectively.

Conversation *is* a core business process and a powerful way for team members to communicate with each other, management, partners, and suppliers and to hold focused and productive discussions.

Conversation *is not* about idle chatter or wasteful talk.

Conversation is basic to how people communicate, yet it seems rare to come out of a conversation feeling as if you have gained an insight or made a commitment that would fundamentally make a difference to the parties involved. Some people believe that we should "stop talking and get some work done." This grows out of a concern that talking is not productive—and in fact it may not be if the parties do not share the values and techniques highlighted in these toolsets.

Embrace these points of view:

1. Conversation is a core business process and should be treated as such.

2. Asking questions that matter, without alienating the people you are asking, is an important tool for creating an environment for productive conversation.

3. Organizational learning comes about when people work in an environment of trust (not fear) and when they use dialogue to create a climate of discovery and to focus on how to leverage what is working (rather than to punish people for what is not working).

Think about your typical day. You have too many things going on. Not only that, you are pressured to create greater results, with little input from managers regarding what is important and what they really want. Sound familiar?

You spend the day talking, listening, trying to solve problems, talking some more, writing, going to meetings—often with little actual progress or results. The secret to sustaining effort and achieving project results is a function of effectively managing a vast variety of complex interactions—having a high "interaction quotient" that complements a high technical quotient.

To improve our interactions, we may be exhorted to think outside the box. But the boxes guiding our conversations are not visible, nor can we think outside them on our own, since our present box (our frame of reference) shapes and influences everything we see, think, and say. In order to think outside the box, we first need to know what box we are in.

Proust writes, "The real voyage of discovery consists not in seeking new landscape but in having new eyes." We need a way of viewing our present box or frame of reference—literally new eyes!—as a first step to seeing what has worked, what will continue to serve us, and what needs to be addressed if we are to succeed amid today's complexities and new challenges. View dialogue as a way to freely explore the world of ideas. Put yourself in a new frame of reference—either thinking together with others or reflecting by yourself, outside the pressures of project work.

Know that relationships exist in a frame of reference. By changing the frame of reference, you can better lead both yourself and others to achieve greater results or a different outcome. (Refer to the description of the two-circle frame of reference in Chapter 2.)

To deal with conversations involving complaints, Robert Lauridsen and Steven Sherman suggest in *Boss Talk* to reorder the focus or order of conversations in the manner shown in Figure 3-1 and detailed below:

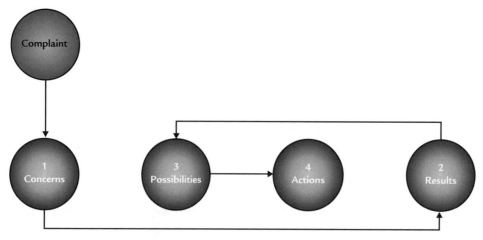

FIGURE 3-1: Refocusing Conversations

Note that a first step when people approach you with complaints is to listen to their concerns. Then, before exploring possibilities and searching for solutions, determine what the desired results are. It could be that the person only wants to vent and know that someone listened. (Some people never want a solution because the problem they love to talk about would be taken away from them.) More often, you need to ascertain if an answer, decision, or steps to take is the desired result. Getting answers to questions about what outcome is needed then refocuses the conversation on discovering viable possibilities. For example, you might ask, "So you think training on the new process would help you avoid those problems in the future?" Then close the conversation with commitment to a course of action.

TOOLSET: COMMITMENT-BASED CONVERSATIONS

When asking for commitments from others, accept only four possible answers:

1. Yes
2. No
3. Negotiated terms (counterproposal)
4. Date when commitment will be made.

(Note that "maybe" is not on this list.)

Everything gets done in language and through conversations. This means work gets done by people making offers, requests, and promises to each other. *Accountability* is how people make promises to deliver on commitments to each other and then either deliver or renegotiate. This is opposed to a slippage culture, where people make promises to deliver to each other and then either deliver or don't deliver.

When any process goes awry, we are left with very few (if any) moves to fix it. We suggest mapping commitments to reveal steps that locate and diagnose breakdowns (e.g., missing requests, missing commitments, lack of agreement on "whats by whens," or absence of designated responsibility) and then intervene to fix them. The ability to map and analyze the value created or destroyed within projects, processes, initiatives, and employee networks is part of outside-the-box thinking.

A leader needs to make an initial assessment of how people and projects within the organization align to goals and execute organizational strategy and then integrate the way people work together. It could be that an effective communication system is lacking; perhaps a strategy exists in stealth mode, invisible to most people; individuals are not collaborating; commitments are loosely conveyed; and promises are not kept. Projects suffer by not delivering on requirements, costing more than budgeted, and taking longer than scheduled. What—or who—is really to blame? All fingers point toward human interactions.

Use the following questions as a means to gauge your interaction quotient:

- Do I believe I am successful and have confidence that I'll continue to be successful?

- Is it possible that as I become more successful, it is harder to deal with feedback that is inconsistent with the way I see myself?

- The more I believe in what got me to where I am, am I more likely to ignore, rationalize, or deny the cues I get from others indicating that I could do better?

- Can I get what I want by operating as usual?
- Are people honoring my requests and delivering to my conditions of satisfaction?
- Am I "in the game," ready to change, wanting to "dance"?

If the assessment of your interaction quotient, goals, and intention are in alignment, you are ready to work toward change. The steps in the process are:

- See a problem (and have exhausted all other options)
- Intend to make change
- Adopt a new perspective
- Do an assessment of the current condition
- Visualize the desired condition
- Implement a new perspective and toolset
- Achieve optimized results.

Use the following set of action steps to begin the process:

- Question: Can I get what I want by operating as usual?
- Ask: Do I intend to change?
- Consider: Do I need to alter my perspective regarding my interaction with others?
- Observe: What is stopping me from acting different?
- Antidote: Increase my ability to observe.
- Request: Over time, notice which frame of reference is sourcing my thoughts, actions, and conversations.
- Practice: Apply new processes and tools.

TOOLSET: ATTITUDE ASSESSMENT

This tool will help you to assess your overall attitude. Carefully select the response on the right that represents your present situation.

1 = All the time or daily   **2** = Frequently   **3** = Sometimes   **4** = Rarely   **5** = Never

PART ONE

1.	I watch the news.	1	2	3	4	5
2.	I talk about the news.	1	2	3	4	5
3.	I am affected by, or talk about, bad weather.	1	2	3	4	5
4.	I am mad at someone for more than one hour.	1	2	3	4	5
5.	When something goes wrong, I blame others.	1	2	3	4	5
6.	When something goes wrong, I dwell on self-blame.	1	2	3	4	5
7.	I bring my problems to work.	1	2	3	4	5
8.	I talk about my problems at work.	1	2	3	4	5
9.	I take my work problems home.	1	2	3	4	5

PART TWO

Read closely: the numeric values of the responses reverse in this part.

1 = Never   **2** = Rarely   **3** = Sometimes   **4** = Frequently   **5** = All the time

1.	I am an enthusiastic project manager.	1	2	3	4	5
2.	I am happy on the inside.	1	2	3	4	5
3.	I look for the good in things.	1	2	3	4	5
4.	I usually talk about the good in things.	1	2	3	4	5
5.	I say why I like things and people, not why I don't.	1	2	3	4	5
6.	I look for opportunities when something bad happens.	1	2	3	4	5
7.	I forgive people who have hurt or offended me.	1	2	3	4	5
8.	If I have nothing nice to say, I say nothing.	1	2	3	4	5
9.	I encourage myself.	1	2	3	4	5
10.	I use positive attitude language. I avoid *can't* and *won't*.	1	2	3	4	5
11.	I have a positive self-image.	1	2	3	4	5

12. I exercise choices that build my positive attitude.   1   2   3   4   5

13. I help others without expectation or measuring.   1   2   3   4   5

14. I am more motivated to help people than I am
    to make money.   1   2   3   4   5

15. I often encourage others to succeed.   1   2   3   4   5

16. I am happy about myself and my life.   1   2   3   4   5

17. I work on my attitude every day.   1   2   3   4   5

18. I listen to attitude audio resources, and
    I attend seminars that relate to attitude.   1   2   3   4   5

19. I ignore people who try to discourage me or tell me
    "you cannot."   1   2   3   4   5

20. I count my blessings every day.   1   2   3   4   5

21. I believe in myself.   1   2   3   4   5

How to calculate your score:

First, count the number of 1s that you selected in Part One and put them on the line next to 1x under Part One on the following page. Do the same for the 2s, 3s, 4s, and 5s you selected, and repeat this process for Part Two.

To calculate your total, multiply the left (1x, 2x) number by the number you wrote on the line, add your numbers from the right-hand columns to get your Part One total score and your Part Two total score, and add your Part One total score and your Part Two total score to get your total score for the assessment.

PART ONE

1 x _____ = _____

2 x _____ = _____

3 x _____ = _____

4 x _____ = _____

5 x _____ = _____

PART ONE Total Score _____

PART TWO

1 x _____ = _____

2 x _____ = _____

3 x _____ = _____

4 x _____ = _____

5 x _____ = _____

PART TWO Total Score _____

TOTAL SCORE _____

How positive is your attitude?

Scoring	Meaning
135–150	You have a positive attitude and confidence in your abilities.
120–134	You have a good attitude and understand what it will take to improve. Go for the gold!
75–119	You are in the big club of people who think they have a positive attitude—but don't. You are in need of skill-building help and need to work actively on attitude exercises every day.
50–74	You have a negative attitude. Read several books on attitude. Change your work and personal habits as part of your skill building. Don't give up.
29–49	You have a lot of work to do—better get started now.

TOOLSET: ATTITUDE ACTIONS

We share the following suggestions based on our experiences managing projects in various organizations worldwide. You may be tempted to say these practices are not valid for you. We ask that you suspend that thinking and give them a try.

- **Admit it is no one's fault but yours.** The more you blame others—your team members, your sponsor, or other project stakeholders—the less chance you have to think positive thoughts, think about an alternative or potential solution, and take positive action toward a solution. The opposite of blame is responsibility. Your first responsibility is to control your thoughts. You cannot avoid project issues and problems, but when the fault is your own, recognize it.

- **Understand that you always have a choice.** Your attitude is a choice, and many people choose negativity. Why? It is more natural to blame and defend than it is to admit and take responsibility. Team members observe your reactions, so be careful about what you do in front of others.

- **If you think it is okay, it is**—and if you think it is not okay, it is not. Your thoughts direct your attitude to a path. If you think "This is crappy," or "Why does this always happen to me?" you have chosen a negative path. If you instead think "This may not be greatest, but look what I'm learning," you have chosen a positive path.

- **Invest your time, do not spend it**. Manage your professional career like a project. Invest an hour each day in developing one needed skill as a project manager. In five to ten years, you will become a world-class expert. Reading books and listening to CDs are positive ways to get started, but you also need to put the ideas you learn into practice in the projects you manage.

- **Study the thoughts and writings of positive people.** If you do not have positive colleagues around you, read material from authors like Norman Vincent Peale. His words are really priceless.

- **Attend seminars and take courses on attitude.** Look at the offerings of any local school or university and find an "attitude course." The Project Management Institute offers many soft-skill seminar experiences and knowledge. Focus on learning about your patterns and reactions, and prepare a plan to improve.

- **Check your language.** Do you say "half full" or "half empty?" They are just words, but they are a reflection of how your mind sees things and an indication of how you process thoughts. How do you answer somebody who asks how you are—positively or negatively?

- **Avoid negative words.** The worst ones are *can't* and *won't*. When I worked for HP, I (Bucero) had a colleague who told me, "Alfonso, please never say *I cannot*; try it, fail, learn and try it again." That sentence changed my life as a project manager.

- **Say why you like things and people, not why you don't.** I like my project manager job because I love dealing with people and issues. I like my attitude because…. Make enough positive statements, and doing so will become a habit. However, you need a lot of practice.

- **Help others, but without expectation or measuring.** If you think someone "owes you one," you are counting or measuring. If you give help away freely, you do not ever have to worry about the measurement. The world will reward you ten times over.

- **Think about your winning and losing words.** Be aware of "loser" phrases and expressions. We see people saying things like, "I always fail when I deliver a sales presentation." Do not do that. Analyze why that happens and make a plan to improve.

- **Think about your mood and your mood swings.** How long do you stay in a bad mood? If it is more than five minutes, something is wrong. Over time, your attitude, your relationships, your results, and your success will suffer.

- **Are you a complainer?** List the lessons you can learn from those whose success you envy (or resent). This will turn your thinking toward your own success, and away from theirs.

- **Celebrate victory and defeat.** Winning and losing are parts of life—and part of the projects we manage. They are also largely attributable to attitude.

- **Help other project managers who are less prepared than you, and count your blessings every day.** Make the list as long as you can. If you are fortunate enough to have it, start with health.

Are these fifteen best practices the secret to change and to being a positive project manager? We think they come darn close. In my (Bucero) book *Today Is a Good Day*, I tell many personal and professional stories about my experiences with attitude. Everybody can improve their attitude. It is a first step in implementing purposeful change and taking action.

TOOLSET: THINKING POSITIVELY

As youngsters, we knew we had to fall a few times to master any new skill. But as we got older, we started to perceive making mistakes as a bad thing, rather than an essential ingredient in achieving our goal.

Successful people may not particularly enjoy their failures, but they recognize the value of those setbacks. To develop a new skill or reach a target, complete project managers need to be committed to doing what it takes to get there—even if it means putting up with negative feedback or falling on your face now and then.

The Power of Persistence

The key to getting what you want is the willingness to do whatever it takes to accomplish your objective. It's an attitude that says: If it takes five steps to reach my goal, I'll take those five steps, but if it takes 30 steps to reach my goal, I will take those 30 steps.

On most occasions in the project field, you don't know how many steps you must take to reach your goal or to accomplish your deliverables.

Here is a set of ten checklist rules to help you become a more persistent project manager:

☐ 1. **I will have no regrets.** Even if the desired result does not come about, I know I tried my best.

☐ 2. **I will achieve my dreams through small actions.** I don't need to take major action each day. Even little steps will bring me closer to my goal.

☐ 3. **I will live in the moment.** I won't focus on the past or dwell too much on the future.

☐ 4. **I will keep my goals in sight.** To keep my vision front and center, I will carry a written copy of my goals and review them every day.

☐ 5. **I realize I will encounter obstacles.** Goals lie behind stumbling blocks. If I can't vault over these obstacles, I will maneuver around them.

☐ 6. **I will focus on one or two goals only.** Too many objectives dissipate energy, and loss of energy is followed by loss of persistence.

☐ 7. **I will trust myself.** If others can do it, so can I. I know all the power to achieve my goals lies within me.

☐ 8. **I will take a break every now and then.** After every success, no matter how slight, I will let myself rest and then get back on the job rejuvenated.

☐ 9. **I will be flexible.** Sometimes I have to break with traditional processes.

☐ 10. **I will be patient.** Time defeats persistence. It is my greatest friend and my greatest enemy.

TOOLSET: PROJECT MANAGEMENT APTITUDE EXERCISE

Answer "true" or "false" to the items below. Be honest and critical in your self-evaluation.

	True	False
You don't plan well because you consider yourself a doer rather than a planner. Many people consider themselves action oriented. When they are given an assignment, their first tendency is to jump in and solve the problem. (Even though planning can be a form of doing, let us make a distinction between the two for the purposes of this example.)		
You manage with minimal collaboration and interaction with customers and team members. This is the classic case of the individual who feels more comfortable working alone. Many people are more productive this way. This person works by him- or herself on the project plan, hands out work assignments, and validates that the work is done. He or she tends to be uncomfortable with a lot of human interaction.		
You tend to make excuses for problems rather than take responsibility. Some project managers understand that they are responsible for most of what goes on within a project. To others, there is always a logical reason why things do not get done. What is your habit? Do you try to explain problems away, or do you take responsibility for the good and the bad and strive to eliminate the causes of problems and failures?		
You are an order-taker for your business client, and you do not use scope change management. Do you think that client-focused behavior means that you take on whatever the client wants? Or do you invoke scope change processes to manage changes?		

	True	False
You let problems sit until they become disasters. Let's face it. There are many procrastinators among us. Do you consider project problems to be nuisances that you hope will go away? Do you focus on problems only after they start to affect the project?		
You don't create a work plan, or you don't keep it up to date. This is common on many projects. Many project managers go through the exercise of creating a project work plan, but then they never update it, or they abandon it somewhere during the project life cycle. If they are asked how much work remains, they have a vague idea but they cannot quantify the remaining effort.		
You would rather deliver poor quality than admit you need more time. Many projects finish on time and within budget but only at the expense of quality. The managers of these projects believe they will deliver on time and then fix the problems in production. Are you one of them?		
You spring surprises on people at the last minute rather than manage expectations. Doing this reveals a tendency to be overly optimistic about what can be done in a short time frame or indicates a conscious effort to hide information and hope things work out. Inexperience can lead to unrealistic optimism, but the second possibility, withholding information as part of a deliberate strategy, may be related to a reluctance to communicate.		
You communicate the minimum information required. It is surprising how many project managers think that communication is one of the drudgeries of the job. Their project teams might be making heroic efforts, but these PMs want to put forth the bare minimum when it comes to communicating status. These project managers also do not have regular status meetings. If your project requires extensive communication, would you relish the challenge or be frustrated that others want to know what is going on?		

	True	False
You ignore risks. Some risks are obvious from the start of a project. Other risks show up later while the project is executing. Many project managers do not even consider risk management a part of their project responsibilities. Other managers can identify risk, but they do nothing about it until it is too late.		

Now add up the number of statements you said were true of you. Score yourself as follows:

0—If you did not answer "true" to any of the items, you likely have a good chance of success as a project manager.

1—You are not perfect, but you are not hopeless. Work on the item to which you responded "true" so that you can answer "false" in the future.

2—This is a borderline score (and we are being really charitable here), but you may be able to overcome your deficiencies through additional focus on improving performance in those areas.

More than 2—If you answered "true" to three or more items, you have work to do on your project management mindset. This does not mean you are a bad person. But, given your answers, you need to develop your knowledge of good project management practices or to examine your overall motivation for taking on project management work. Perhaps you can focus on those areas for improvement and take the test again at a later date.

A perfect score does not guarantee perfection as a project manager or even success. However, answering "true" to any of these items reveals a project management deficiency that could place a project at risk—especially larger and more complex projects.

TOOLSET: CREATING AN INFLUENCE MAP

Most project managers need to influence without authority. This tool shows you how to construct an influence map that will help you determine who is influential and how to take advantage of that influence.

There are three main considerations when constructing an influence map:

- The importance or weight of a stakeholder's overall influence (represented by the size of the circle representing that stakeholder).

- The relationships between stakeholders (represented by the presence of lines or arrows between them).

- The amount of influence stakeholders have over others (represented by the heaviness, or width, of the lines drawn between them).

A completed influence map shows the stakeholders with the most influence as individuals with the largest circles. Lines (arrows) drawn to other stakeholders indicate the presence and strength of influence (see Figure 3-2).

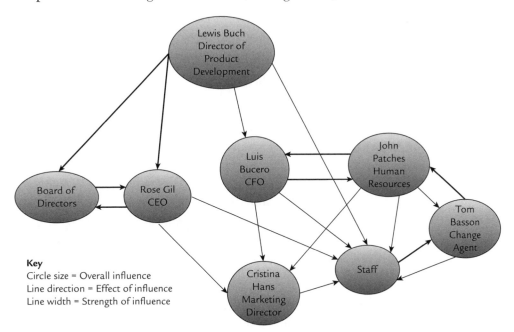

FIGURE 3-2: Influence Map

What To Do	How To Do It
Prepare a stakeholder analysis	Identify project stakeholders and classify them, taking into account their interest and power or influence in the project. This helps to identify, prioritize, and understand key stakeholders.
Gather information on each stakeholder	Whom does he or she influence, and who influences him or her? • How strong is that influence? • What is the history of each relationship? How does this impact overall influence? • What role does hierarchy play in the amount of influence?
Map the importance of influence using the size and position of the circles	The largest circles belong to stakeholders with the most influence. Where possible, place the most influential stakeholders at the top of the page, and put less influential people lower down.
Map the direction of influence by drawing arrows to link the stakeholders	These may be one-way or two-way, depending on whether influence flows to the same extent in both directions.
Map the strength of influence by using thicker lines to indicate stronger influence	Determine influence strength by observing interactions over time or through a questionnaire. In some situations, the person who signs off projects or purchases may not actually be the most influential person in the network. For example, a head of purchasing might always accept the recommendations of the IT department.
Study the map, and identify stakeholders with the most overall influence	Form a stakeholder management plan that allows you to communicate with, and hopefully influence, these important influencers.
Map these influence relationships on a regular basis to better understand the dynamics of decision-making relating to the project	Validate the map with others who are familiar with the people involved.

TOOLSET: CREATE A PERSONAL NETWORKING PLAN

Professional networking is also a project, so prepare a plan for that project. It is critical to clearly identify network contacts, develop a personalized networking plan, and build an administrative process to manage it all. It is very important to ask network contacts for their help, not for a job. People are delighted to help, but few will have a job to offer.

1. First-level contacts: These are the hottest prospects and people you know best— current and past colleagues and managers, vendors, consultants, and recruiters with whom you have an established relationship. Your initial contact will likely be via phone, for instance a quick call announcing you are in the job market and would appreciate advice, assistance, recommendations, or referrals.

   At the end of each conversation, tell your contacts you would like to send them a resume to have on file and ask if they prefer mail, fax, or email. Immediately forward your resume with a brief, friendly cover letter, thanking them for any help they can offer and mentioning the positions and industries in which you are interested.

   If you have not heard back from contacts within three weeks, call and inquire if they have reviewed your resume and if they have any recommendations.

2. Second-level contacts: These are people you know casually. Your initial contact will most likely be 50 percent by phone and 50 percent by mail or email, depending on how comfortable you are in these relationships and how easy it is to connect with each individual. Whenever possible, it is best if the initial contact is a phone call, allowing you to establish a more personal relationship. If you have called a contact, follow up immediately by sending a resume. If you have not heard back from contacts within three weeks, call or email them and inquire if they have reviewed your resume and if they have any recommendations.

Once you have developed your list of contacts and determined how to connect with each individual, set up a system to track all calls, contacts, and follow-up commitments.

TOOLSET: AVOID NETWORKING GAFFES

1. **Choose among the favors that others offer.** Do not jump at every offer to join a professional network.

2. **Understand the culture and rules at the sites where others work.** Before contacting colleagues of the friend who invited you to a networking group, get to know the group's culture.

3. **Hone your profile.** Review your profile and underline the characteristics you most want to highlight to other people.

4. **Do not be pushy.** Most professional networks do not like arrogant people.

5. **Do what you say you will.** Practice authenticity and integrity.

6. **Prepare for face-to-face introductions.** A face-to-face meeting requires you to respond spontaneously, without the time afforded by email to craft your message. Also, it is important to decide what you want from a meeting ahead of time.

7. **Help yourself by helping others.** Networking is reciprocal, so do unto others as you want done to you. If you are able to help people, they will be more likely to remember you and return the favor.

Figure 3-3 illustrates these tips.

FIGURE 3-3: Best Practices for Networking

TOOLSET: HOW TO DEVELOP YOUR POTENTIAL AS A PROJECT MANAGER

Complete project managers want the satisfaction of knowing they are making the most of their potential. To be successful in your own eyes and in the eyes of other project stakeholders, pay attention to these twelve basic traits we uncovered via interviews among European colleagues:

1. **Common sense.** Brush away extraneous, irrelevant thoughts and ideas to get at the core of what matters. All professionals interviewed agreed on this subject, with a Spanish colleague commenting that "common sense is the less common of all the senses in project management."

2. **Specialized knowledge of your field.** Make an effort to keep learning constantly throughout projects. Knowing what you are doing reduces the risks and works like an insurance policy for your own stability within an existing work environment. Most Europeans have a desire for security and continuity as part of their culture.

3. **Self-reliance.** Have the courage to get things moving by relying primarily on your own resources and abilities and exerting plain old willpower.

4. **General intelligence.** The professionals interviewed say this includes an extensive vocabulary as well as good oral and written skills. European project managers are more and more focused on soft-skills development. Intercultural training is also becoming more popular in European countries such as Spain.

5. **Ability to get things done.** Successful project managers have strong organizational abilities and productive work habits and can distinguish between what is important and what is not.

6. **Leadership.** Think motivation, not intimidation. An effective leadership style combines a blend of discipline and flexibility. Managing the effects of globalization and dealing with people as human beings, regardless of nationality or origin, are important for all professionals.

7. **Knowing right from wrong.** Be sensitive to moral and ethical concerns—and be politically savvy. Understand your local project environment, acting locally and thinking globally.

8. **Creativity.** Natural talent plus insight or intuition is equal to creativity. Natural gifts are not, however, as important as making the best use of your abilities.

9. **Self-confidence.** This feeling of assurance is based on knowing you have done everything possible to prepare. Europeans have the feeling that all people have weaknesses and sometimes one just has to muddle through life.

10. **Oral expression.** Successful project managers can get their message across, even in front of a large group.

11. **Concern for others.** At the very least, successful project managers can get along with others.

12. **Luck** always helps, but it is never enough.

TOOLSET: LEADERSHIP COMPETENCIES–EMOTIONAL INTELLIGENCE

Score each item from 1 to 10. 1 means "never"; 10 means "always."

☐ 1. I carefully read my own emotions and recognize their impact; I use "gut sense" to guide decisions.

☐ 2. I know my strengths and limits.

☐ 3. I have a sound sense of my self-worth and capabilities.

☐ 4. I keep disruptive emotions and impulses under control.

☐ 5. I display honesty and integrity and am highly trustworthy.

☐ 6. I am flexible in adapting to changing situations or overcoming obstacles.

☐ 7. I have a high drive to improve performance to meet my inner standards of excellence.

☐ 8. I readily act and seize opportunities.

☐ 9. I see the upside in events.

☐ 10. I can sense others' emotions and understand their perspective, and I take active interest in their concerns.

☐ 11. I can read the currents, decision networks, and politics at the organizational level.

☐ 12. I recognize and meet colleague, client, or customer needs.

☐ 13. I guide and motivate others with a compelling vision.

☐ 14. I wield a range of tactics for persuasion.

☐ 15. I bolster others' abilities through feedback and guidance.

☐ 16. I initiate, manage, and lead others in new directions.

☐ 17. I skillfully resolve disagreements.

☐ 18. I have strong cooperation and team-building skills.

Map your scores into the next toolset, Emotional Intelligence Domains and Associated Competencies.

TOOLSET: EMOTIONAL INTELLIGENCE DOMAINS AND ASSOCIATED COMPETENCIES

This toolset is based upon *Primal Leadership* by Daniel Goleman, Richard Boyatzis, and Annie McKee.

"Effective leaders typically demonstrate strengths in at least one competence from each of the four fundamental areas of emotional intelligence" (2002, p. 40).

- **Self-awareness:** Can I accurately identify my own emotions as they happen and tendencies as I express them?

- **Self-management:** Can I manage my emotions and behavior to achieve a positive outcome?

- **Social awareness:** Can I accurately identify your emotions and tendencies as I interact with you or a group?

- **Relationship management:** Can I manage the interactions I have with others constructively and to a positive outcome?

	What I See	**What I Do**
Personal Competence	Self-Awareness	Self-Management
Social Competence	Social Awareness	Relationship Management

Each numbered item from the Leadership Competencies–Emotional Intelligence toolset corresponds to a specific component of emotional intelligence as listed below. For example, item 1 is related to emotional self-awareness, item 2 to accurate self-assessment.

Map your scores from the toolset to the four areas of emotional intelligence by writing your score for each item next to the relevant component of emotional intelligence.

PERSONAL COMPETENCE

Self-awareness: Can I accurately identify my own emotions as they happen and tendencies as I express them?

☐ 1.   Emotional self-awareness

☐ 2.   Accurate self-assessment

☐ 3.   Self-confidence

Self-management: Can I manage my emotions and behavior to achieve a positive outcome?

☐ 4.   Emotional self-control

☐ 5.   Transparency

☐ 6.   Adaptability

☐ 7.   Achievement

☐ 8.   Initiative

☐ 9.   Optimism

SOCIAL COMPETENCE

Social awareness: Can I accurately identify your emotions and tendencies as I interact with you or a group?

☐ 10. Empathy

☐ 11. Organizational awareness

☐ 12. Service

Relationship management: Can I manage the interactions I have with others constructively and to a positive outcome?

☐ 13. Inspirational leadership

☐ 14. Influence

☐ 15. Developing others

☐ 16. Change catalyst

☐ 17. Conflict management

☐ 18. Teamwork and collaboration

Assess your areas of strength and the best practices you employ to achieve those high scores. Continue or expand these practices and share them with others. For areas in which your scores are lower, seek out others with high scores and probe for practices they use that you can emulate.

TOOLSET: WINNING WORDS OF WISDOM

Complete project managers are always on the lookout for gems or nuggets of truth that inspire them or others in their quest for excellence. Coach Vince Lombardi said, "The quality of our lives is in direct proportion to our commitment to excellence." Michael Levine (1996) of Levine Communications provided this set of guidelines:

- Live your life in the manner that you would like your children to live theirs.
- You know you're doing something right when you start being copied.
- Extraordinary people are most often ordinary people with extraordinary determination.
- Many important battles in life have to be fought more than once to be won.
- We must train ourselves not to see the world through only our own eyes.
- When choosing a career, the trick is to find a job that you would do for free if life afforded you that opportunity.
- The job of a manager is not to do everything—it is to make sure that every task gets done.
- The only job security in the world is to be more talented tomorrow than you are today.
- Nothing is as stressful as trying to be a different person from who you are.
- A pessimist is someone who complains about the noise when opportunity knocks.
- As a leader, you must constantly change the definition of winning. Keep moving the goal posts.

TOOLSET: PERSONAL SKILLS–APPLYING A TEMPLATE FOR SUCCESS

Over the years I (Englund) have been blessed and enlightened by personal stories told by co-author and cultural anthropologist Dr. Robert J. Graham. During a dinnertime conversation, he described the ingenious process he used to succeed in a seemingly impossible situation. The following essay is a simple to understand yet powerful template for success in any endeavor—and it demonstrates the power of storytelling to illustrate key concepts.

Prologue

It was January of 1966, and I needed to register for the second semester of my sophomore year in college. I was attending a local state college outside Philadelphia, but I was not happy with the courses suggested for my curriculum. Only one or two of the suggested courses were of any interest to me. But since I had to register for something, I decided to read the entire catalog to see if there were any five courses that interested me. While reading through the mathematics department offerings, I saw there were two courses offered regarding how to use a computer. The first was an introductory course available to college juniors, and the second was an advanced course open to senior mathematics majors only. I was neither a junior, nor a senior, nor a math major, but the courses looked interesting, so I signed up anyway. I found the courses to be quite fascinating, and so I asked one of the instructors if any more computer courses would be offered the next year. He said no but then told me that he had just read about a college somewhere in Ohio that had just started a curriculum in systems analysis. We looked it up and I wrote away for some information.

Achieving the Impossible

When I received the information, two things became very clear. The first was that the curriculum was exactly what I wanted. The second thing was that, unfortunately, there was no way that I qualified for that school. This was a serious place that only accepted people from the top 20 percent of the graduating class in Ohio. If you wanted to apply from outside of Ohio, as I did, your high school rank had to be much higher than that. My high school rank was in the bottom 20 percent, and from a mediocre high school to boot. If you wanted to transfer, as I did, they wanted to see at least a 2.8 GPA from your existing college. I was barely staying in school, with a GPA just above 2.0.

There were several reasons why I was doing so poorly. The first was that I lacked any focus or direction in my studies. The second was that I had vaguely seen myself as making a living in the music business and, as a result, I was spending all my time playing and singing in a local rock-and-roll band. This meant that I was staying up to about 3 a.m., playing in sleazy bars in Philadelphia, then attempting to stay awake in class the next day. This was not the life of a serious student. So even though the school's curriculum seemed to offer me some focus and direction in my studies, the total of my academic experiences did not indicate that I could ever be admitted to study the curriculum.

The Dean

I continued to read through the material, and I saw a note saying that the dean of the School of Applied Science would occasionally have Saturday morning office hours where students could make appointments to talk to him. I began to think that if I could get to see him I might be able to convince him to let me into the school. It was a long shot, but it looked like the only shot I had. So I wrote away to the dean telling him that I wanted to transfer into the program and asked if I could come out to the school to talk to him about it. Amazingly, I got the appointment, one Saturday morning a few weeks hence.

Before meeting with the dean, I did a bit of soul-searching and found that indeed I had the confidence that I could succeed at the school if the dean would just let me in. I also realized that to do that, I had to change my ways, drastically. So when the day came I laid my story in front of the dean and told him that if he would let me into the school for just one year that I would quit the band, sell my instruments, and hit the books. To my astonishment, he went for the deal. Three weeks later I got the thick envelope. I had achieved the impossible. So I quit the band, sold my instruments, moved to Ohio, and hit the books—hard.

Epilogue

I graduated in 1969. I took a job directing the computer center for Thomas More College in northern Kentucky, enrolled in a graduate program in operations research in the business school at the University of Cincinnati, and received an MBA in 1971 and Ph.D. in 1974. As I was nearing completion of my Ph.D., I actually had talks with the people in the systems analysis department as they tried to convince me to join the faculty there. It was a great offer, but I turned it down because I had engineered an even better offer for a postdoctoral fellowship at the Wharton School at the University of Pennsylvania, working with one of the founders of the field of operations research.

When I got to Penn, I wrote to the dean to tell him the results of his decision. I pointed out that there I was, only eight years after asking him to admit a no-account student, working at one of the top business schools in the world. I wanted to let him know that his decision had worked out well. He wrote back, saying that he did not remember me nor that particular decision, but he added that he must have made the decision based on what he saw standing in front of him that day.

A Template for Success

This experience helped me to develop a process for achieving the impossible. Since I had success the first time I tried it, I have used this template throughout my life.

1. **Clarify your goal.** It is very important to be very clear in your own mind about what you want to achieve and why. This is often the most difficult step. However, if you are not clear in your own mind, there is little chance that you'll be able to convince others to help you. Over time I've found that this step has magic in it. Once you are clear on what you want to achieve, and you commit to your quest, you'll be helped along by all manner of people, many of whom you don't even know exist when your quest begins.

2. **Do it.** Even though the odds are long, even if your friends tell you it will never work, you've got to take the journey. Every organization has a variety of ways to get in, much the same as every building has a side door or a back door. If you feel you can't get into the front door, then search for the side door. Be positive and believe that the door is indeed there. This may take a lot of time, but if the goal is worthwhile, it will be time well spent.

3. **Show up!** This is extremely important. The impossible cannot be achieved by mail or telephone. Remember the reply from the dean, who said he made his decision based on what he saw standing in front of him that day. If I were not there to stand in front of him that day, I doubt he would have made the same decision.

Applying the Template

Later on, I was able to use this process to help my daughter get into high school. This was an academically selective high school with a competitive entrance exam. There were two parts to this exam, English and mathematics, and a score of 85 or better was required on each part. She scored 99 on the English part, but only 82 in mathematics. I knew that that 82 did not reflect her true knowledge in math. I discussed this with her and found out that much of the math exam covered geometry. I figured that the reason for the low score was that she learned her geometry in Germany and in the German language, while the exam, of course, was given in English. So the problem she had was not in the concepts of geometry, but rather in the translation of the concepts from German to English. I was absolutely convinced that this was the case, that she knew the material, but in German and not in English. So I had step one of my process for success. All I needed to do was to convince the school board that this was the case.

When I began the quest I had no idea if there was any way to appeal the examination scores. If that were possible, then that would be the side door that I was looking for. Dealing with the bureaucracy of the school board is a daunting task, with little hope of success. I was bounced from department to department, with most people saying they had never heard of such a thing as I was proposing. However, I finally found a person at one department who told me there were five seats that were left open for special cases. The appeal process was available to the principal of the public school that the student attended. The woman at the school board told me she had never heard of a parent initiating an appeal process, nor of it being used for a student from a nonpublic school. But she did tell me I could give it a try by calling the assistant principal at the high school. That was the side door I was looking for, and I was off and running.

I called the assistant principal, who told me that anyone could appeal for those seats as long as they lived in the city. He told me to write up my case and they would consider it. I knew better, and proposed that in addition to writing up the case that we should have a meeting. After all, I argued, this was a "special" special case, and he agreed. The rest was easy. My case was clear, I had found an alternate path, and I showed up.

TOOLSET: BUSINESS IS PERSONAL

Gary R. Heerkens, MBA, CBM, PMP, and president of Management Solutions Group Inc., is a consultant, trainer, speaker, and author of *The Business-Savvy Project Manager*. He writes, "Executives aren't the only ones who should be business-savvy":

> The widespread adoption of a business-driven approach toward projects ultimately relies on executives. It's senior management that has to ensure that practices such as financial analysis and business case preparation become a regular part of doing project business. Inviting the project management community to participate on front-end activities such as strategic planning, operational planning, and portfolio management is largely at their discretion.
>
> That reliance on senior management can be discouraging. However, as an individual project management practitioner, there are some things that you can do to demonstrate your personal knowledge of business. And in some cases, you can advance the cause of business-savvy project management within your organization.

Here are a few examples:

Verify your project is clearly and directly linked to one or more organizational strategies, business objectives, or operational goals. Make sure your managers know you're aware of this linkage and that you will integrate it into your approach toward project decision-making. Speak up if the link is not clear to you.

Understand the business benefits your project yields. For example, does your project advance long-term strategy? Increase revenue? Lower operating costs? Reduce headcount? Increase efficiency? Knowing the big-picture benefits can help your project management approach—but only if you know what you're working toward.

Seek out the right sponsor. Try to determine the person who is at the appropriate level of management and who is viewed as "owning" responsibility for achieving the stated business results. You are likely to learn a great deal and enjoy the support of a manager who offers guidance in making solid, business-based decisions.

Cultivate a working relationship with your organization's financial people. This is particularly helpful if they're regular participants in activities such as project financial analysis. Ask them to teach and help you understand your organization's process.

Recruit a business-minded senior manager as your mentor. Tell him or her that you are striving to bring a business-savvy perspective to your project management. This is one of the best ways to gain useful knowledge while letting you interact with a member of senior management.

Add value. If your organization doesn't currently prepare project business cases, consider drafting one for the next project you are assigned to manage. Present your document to the appropriate managers and suggest that project business case preparation is a valuable procedure they may wish to consider implementing on future project proposals (2011).

In "Getting the Green Light" (2011), Michelle Bowles summarizes the do's and don'ts of building a business case:

DO be prepared. When presenting the business case for a potential project, you must feel confident in your assessments. "As soon as you start struggling to answer an executive's question, you start losing credibility," says Martin Webster, Leicestershire County Council, Leicester, England.

DON'T be afraid to ask for help. If you're pitching a project that will have significant involvement with human resources (HR), for example, enlist coworkers in that department to explain their key concepts and concerns. "The HR colleagues will appreciate that, and it will increase your credibility with executives," Mr. Webster says.

DO get to the bottom line first, only going into the project specifics if requested, says Sinikka Waugh, PMP, Your Clear Next Steps, Indianola, Iowa, USA.

DON'T pitch the project in isolation. If Project A will put Project B at risk by taking away resources, include that information in the business case, Ms. Waugh says.

DO offer alternatives. "A business case for a project should say, 'This is the problem, and this is how we can solve it with different options,'" Mr. Webster says.

DON'T assume executives understand project management speak. "We in the IT project management field use acronyms all the time," Mr. Webster says. "But most executives haven't got a clue what we're talking about. Keep it simple and spell things out." (p. 45)

PROJECT MANAGEMENT SKILLS

TOOLSET: BUILDING A VISION STATEMENT

A project *vision statement* is a vivid description of a desired future state when the project is successful. It is unique to the project. Stakeholders will know when that new state is realized. The statement should be clear, convincing, concise, and compelling. Avoid using jargon, but use terms specific to the project. Craft this statement upon initiating every project.

We advise each project manager to manage his or her career as a project or like a program, starting with a personal vision statement. Each of us manages many projects in our lives, and one of them is our professional development as project managers. A clear vision enables you to achieve great things as a complete project manager.

What To Do	How To Do It
1. Measure yourself.	If you have previously thought about your vision for your project management career and articulated it, measure how well you are carrying it out. Talk to several key people, such as your spouse, a close colleague, and key team members, asking them to state what they think your vision is. If they can articulate it, then you are probably living it.
2. Write it down.	If you have thought about your vision but never put it in writing, take the time to do so today. Writing clarifies your thinking. Once you have written it, evaluate whether it is worthy of your life's best work—and then pursue it with all that you have.

3. Do a gut check.	To improve your vision, spend the next several weeks or months thinking about it. Consider what really impacts you at a gut level. Share the statement with others and see if you get a "Wow!" reaction. Get feedback and make adjustments until the "Wow" metric is met.
4. What makes you cry?	Examples: being alone, not being able to delegate, not having money for hiring new people, not growing as a company. (These do not have to be things that literally make you cry, just things that trouble you.) What future state of being would make these things disappear?
5. What makes you dream?	Examples: your business, your enthusiasm, your results, your future. How can you incorporate them into your vision?
6. What gives you energy?	Examples: writing, speaking, and consulting in your field of expertise (project management). Leading teams and making things happen. Motivating and encouraging people. Building up your professional career. Seeing things working the way you intended. Craft a vision that involves doing more of these things.

TOOLSET: RESOURCE PLANNING CHECKLIST

Although the project sponsor and steering committee are ultimately responsible for assigning scarce resources, it is important for the project leader to demonstrate the consequences to the project deadline or quality if the necessary resources are not obtained. Involve the project steering committee or project sponsor in the decision-making process for resource utilization.

Do an analysis of all key people who have a stake in the project in order to:

What To Do	How To Do It
Understand	Assess and understand the real human resource needs for the project.
Establish expectations	Define accountability measures and performance expectations for all resources.
Recognize	Recognize all issues and concerns regarding human resources and make them visible to the project sponsor.
Identify	Identify preferred communication processes for each stakeholder.
Mitigate	Mitigate potential conflicts regarding elements such as availability, opposing priorities, personalities, and skill levels.
Develop	Develop collaboration mindsets such that resources form loyalties and accountabilities for the project or program.

TOOLSET: STAKEHOLDER ANALYSIS

Stakeholder analysis helps us understand how different individuals can influence decision-making throughout a project. To perform your own stakeholder analysis, ask the following four basic questions, and follow a process similar to the one outlined below.

a) Who are our stakeholders?

1. The project team brainstormed to identify all possible stakeholders.

2. We identified where each of the stakeholders was located.

3. We identified the relationships the project team had with each of the stakeholders.

b) What are the stakeholders' expectations?

4. For each stakeholder, we identified their primary project expectations at a high level.

c) How does the project (or products) affect the stakeholders?

5. We analyzed how the products and deliverables were affecting each of the stakeholders.

6. We determined the actions each stakeholder could take that would affect the success or failure of the project.

7. We prioritized the stakeholders based on who had the greatest potential effect, positive or negative, on project success or failure.

8. We also incorporated information from the previous steps into a risk analysis plan to develop mitigation procedures for stakeholders who might negatively impact the project.

d) What information do stakeholders need?

9. We identified from the information collected in previous steps what information needed to be furnished each of them, when should it be provided, and how.

TOOLSET: CONTROL OR RESULTS EXERCISE

One way to get a group or team to think about control versus results—especially in advance of when a conflict arises—is to conduct a knowledge café exercise. In workshops for PMI SeminarsWorld, we have small teams address each of the topic questions by starting with one question and brainstorming their responses, then moving on to another topic and building upon previous responses. The role of each team in the third rotation is to summarize all comments.

Directions

Write one of the following topics at the top of a flip chart.

- When do you feel in control?
- How do you know when you are getting results?
- What constitutes optimum controls for desired results?

Brainstorm the topic and record your team's response on the flip chart (approximately 10 minutes).

Rotate (clockwise) to the next chart. Brainstorm the new topic and add your responses (approximately 5 minutes).

Rotate (clockwise) to the next chart. Review the information on the flip chart, brainstorm, summarize key points, and record your responses (approximately 10 minutes). Debrief the topic in summary form.

TABLE 4-1:   Sample Responses to the Control or Results Exercise

I feel in control when:
•   I receive reliable information
•   Enough information is available to make the right decision
•   My decisions directly affect the outcomes
I know I am getting good results when:
•   Processes are working
•   Key performance indicators (KPIs) and milestones are being met
•   The customer is smiling
Optimum controls for desired results are:
•   Clearly defined goals with just enough process and measures
•   Right level and cost relative to size and complexity
•   Controls help, not hinder progress

Table 4-1 summarizes responses from typical workshop sessions. This group achieved the objective of identifying specific actions that help them achieve both control and results, while at the same time realizing both may not be possible or trade-offs may be required. The group identified that feedback mechanisms and rapid response to variances are necessary. Further refinements of this exercise will revolve around helping people articulate their values when conflict arises.

The value of this exercise for project teams or business steering committees is that it facilitates reflection and dialogue. The intent is to surface cultural or other values that provide clues—or forewarnings—about how the organization will react to inevitable crises. This exercise is an adjunct to, and does not replace, the need to gain clarity regarding a project's vision, mission, goals, and objectives. The exercise may also reveal that a project's intended results are not well defined and need additional clarification.

TOOLSET: MONITORING AND CONTROLLING PROJECT WORK USING A WORK-STYLE METRIC

Drawing from his long and varied career in both commercial and government organizations, Thomas J. Buckholtz shared with us these tools he developed as "a work-style metric for improving project management, specific work, and working culture":

> Because monitoring and controlling project work is the process of tracking, reviewing, and regulating progress to meet performance objectives in the project management plan, including the implementation of corrective or preventive actions to bring the project into compliance with the plan when variances occur, a need arises to measure task completion and comparison with plan. The following description of a work-style metric may assist, especially at a high-level view, in assessing how well work is progressing and what level of maturity is present. It also helps determine if an organization's existing processes make it ready for change.

Use the work-style metric presented in this toolset for purposes such as:
- Measuring one dimension of how work is being done. Work can include specific tasks, entire projects, project management, and attempts to improve any of the previous items.
- Pinpointing and evaluating opportunities regarding how well work should be done. Opportunities can include changing work styles and improving work within its existing styles.
- Determining work-style match or mismatch between one individual or team and the needs of a project or the styles of another individual or team.

Work style can be measured on a scale that includes the following (Buckholtz 2011):
- **Pending:** Task owners are not performing the work, even though outcomes the work can produce are needed.
- **Ad Hoc:** Task owners try to perform the work without using processes.
- **Experimental:** Task owners try various processes.
- **Routine:** Task owners follow established processes.
- **Obviated:** Task owners do not perform the work, because performing it is not needed.

The following scenario-exercises indicate uses of this metric.

1. An advisor to a startup software company has experience indicating the potential for rapidly developing high-quality software by using Routine and Obviated

coding and testing processes that are based on developing and using software-development tools. The company's software development team uses Ad Hoc coding and testing practices.

– **Exercise:** Under what circumstances should the advisor advocate changing the company's software-development practices?

– **Example:** The company's leadership did not exhibit much Routine behavior. The company was unlikely to be able to hire Experimental or Routine programmers and might, if it tried to change development style, lose its developers. The advisor did not emphasize the possibility of improving software-development productivity.

2. A chief information officer (CIO) pushes the information-technology department (a) to help people throughout an enterprise perform work with Routine style and (b) to automate work (Obviated, for people's work). The CIO's department strives to make its services reliable and its own work Routine.

– **Exercise:** What risks accrue to the enterprise from these behaviors?

– **Example:** The information technology (IT) department ignored new Ad Hoc and Experimental technologies that might have helped people change from Pending or Ad Hoc behavior, for some types of work, to Ad Hoc or Experimental styles, respectively. Units outside the IT department adopted, on their own, the new technology. Later, the enterprise expended considerable effort to harmonize and integrate work processes and technologies.

– **Example:** A similar enterprise maintained an advanced-technology function within its IT department. For the same new technology, the IT department and the rest of the enterprise worked together, from the very first use of the new technologies. The enterprise streamlined work and reduced costs. New technology was selected, acquired, and deployed efficiently and cost-effectively.

3. A large organization finds it difficult to grow new lines of business.

– **Exercise:** Determine to what extent this difficulty can be attributed to …

   a. Attitudes that it takes too long for new lines of business to become financially significant?

   b. Other factors?

– **Example:** Key people working in the established lines of business had suspicions about products, services, and work that were mostly not Routine.

4. People complain about bureaucracy.

– **Exercise:** To what extent do the Routine aspects of bureaucratic work free up time and other resources to do innovative work?

– **Example:** In a large organization, people followed processes and precedents for Routine work, thereby having time to develop Experimental and even Routine approaches to innovation.

5. People praise the high degree to which an enterprise's work has become Routine and even (for people) Obviated by automation.
    - **Exercise:** To what extent does dependence on automation decrease abilities to cope with disasters, cyber-attacks, or other emergencies?
    - **Example:** A company maintained its own telecommunications system, independent of traditional public providers, and thereby exhibited aspects of Experimental behavior.

Depending on the context in which work is being done, each style can represent potential strengths and potential weaknesses. For example:

- Pending
    - Possible strength: Planning is appropriate, but doing is not.
    - Possible weakness: Needed work is not getting done.

- Ad Hoc
    - Possible strength: Spontaneity promotes creativity.
    - Possible weakness: Efficiency and effectiveness are lacking.

- Experimental
    - Possible strength: Processes improve methodically.
    - Possible weakness: People focus too much on process and not enough on results.

- Routine
    - Possible strength: Work proceeds efficiently.
    - Possible weakness: Flexibility or creativity is stifled.

- Obviated
    - Possible strength: People focus on other activities.
    - Possible weakness: People lack or lose abilities to perform activities (Buckholtz 2007).

When you notice that some work significantly exhibits more than one style, consider assessing the styles of significant components of the work.

Check out Buckholtz (2011), which includes a service-functionality (or service-value) metric, examples using each of the two metrics, and references to publications discussing similar topics, as well as Buckholtz (2007), which includes similar style and functionality tools, other Direct Outcomes systems-thinking tools, and examples of how each tool can be used.

TOOLSET: METRICS STRATEGY

Gustav Toppenberg, a senior PMO manager in Cisco's Communication & Collaboration IT group, is responsible for leading the PMO and driving project and operational excellence within his team and across the organization. Gustav has led projects in change leadership, acquisition integration, and globalization strategy. He is also involved in Cisco IT's transition to a services-oriented organization (technology, process, and culture), enabling a client-focused, value-driven, cost-effective alignment between IT and business.

With a background in strategy consulting, program/project management, and global change management, Gustav has an interest in and passion for the convergence of business and technology. He is a natural change leader and constant disruptor. He continuously seeks to occupy the gap between business and technology, thereby leveraging technology solutions to strengthen competitive advantages in business. These traits are increasingly representative of a complete project manager.

Gustav offers these suggestions for defining and driving a realistic metrics strategy and covers the risks and benefits of using metrics:

> No matter what your role is in the project organization and whether you are just starting to define your framework and strategy or have a well-developed one in place, ensuring that you have a continuous understanding of the risks and benefits is paramount to how successful your results will be.
>
> In various versions we have heard the old adage "What gets measured gets done." It has been attributed to thought leaders such as Peter Drucker, Tom Peters, Edwards Deming, Lord Kelvin, and others. Peter Drucker expanded on the above and said, "What gets measured, gets managed." If this is true, then it is paramount that before measuring something, you need to understand what it is you are attempting to "do" or "manage." Each metric that is established needs to influence and change a behavior in the organization, and that changed behavior is key to implementing a strategic framework.
>
> Before assessing the benefits and risks of metrics, we must first understand how to define what is being measured. Following are five concepts to consider when defining metrics:
>
> **Metrics need to be:**
> 1. **Objective.** Ensure that the metric is not dependent on a human influence; create the metric so that it is driven by objective monitoring and measurement. Examples of this abound in various environments, and it is crucial that continuous monitoring ensures that there is little opportunity for influence or gaming.

2. **Predictive/repeatable**—both the metric itself and the behavior being modified. Ensure that the definition of the metric allows enough specificity to zero in on the issues and ensure that it is something that has a trend to it. Associated behaviors by people in the organization are linked to these trends. As you monitor and control the measurement, you also modify the behavior, but be patient; it doesn't happen overnight.

3. **Automated.** Striving for automation of metrics will help accomplish two critical elements. The first is minimizing the influence of stakeholders in the results of the measurements; the second is the time sink the collection of data and analysis to derive information can take. The more automation you can leverage, the more time you can spend refining the strategy and achieving alignment to the company's strategy.

4. **Actionable.** Enact the KISS (keep it short and simple) principle when choosing metrics; don't boil the ocean. As you start to inventory current metrics, you tend to latch on to every metric you can get your hands on. But, if you focus on those metrics that drive actionable change and behavior modification aligned with the company's strategy, you are much more likely to succeed.

5. **Leading vs. lagging.** While learning from past performance can be helpful, focusing on predicting future trends is much more powerful. Good metrics have a balance of both; focus on asking questions about what you want to "do" or "manage" and how it will look in the future. Picking leading-indicators metrics that help paint that picture will keep you well informed and positioned for success.

Once metrics are defined or refined, it is time to think of risks and benefits that come with a metrics framework strategy. Here are some of the most impactful:

Risk: The human fudge factor. Keeping the metric free of human interest and influence is important to ensure the metric is believable and the process is transparent. To develop the metric and ensure adoption to drive behavior change, however, the metric owner needs to help design the metric to ensure it makes sense.

Risk: Driving a different behavior than planned. The most well-designed metric can have a much different effect than anticipated, especially when mixed into the broader enterprise environment.

Risk: Academic versus practical. When designing metrics, involve the metric owner to ensure that the metric is practical to implement. Excellent sources are out there to help identify industry-standard metrics—take the time to mold them to fit particular situations.

Benefit: Benchmarking. If you choose metrics that your competitors and partners are using, you can easily benchmark against them or your industry to keep on track.

Benefit: Visibility and transparency through metrics, if well developed, communicated, and adopted, should remove the emotional barriers to having constructive conversations about the direction the project, program, or portfolio is heading and how to course-correct.

Benefit: Ensuring that projects and programs are aligned to the company's strategy and enable it to be executed or alert you to any inconsistencies in the intended execution.

TOOLSET: THE BASICS OF SIX SIGMA

Sandra A. Swanson (2011) writes that the goal of the management philosophy Six Sigma is to achieve 99.9997 percent reliability. In an effort to reduce product defects to a mere 3.4 per million, Motorola, the telecom company in Schaumburg, Illinois, developed Six Sigma in the mid-1980s. The manufacturer achieved that level of reliability, thanks in part to a rigorous focus on data gathering and statistical analysis.

Pairing Six Sigma with project management best practices effectively improves an array of business processes. At its core is a process called DMAIC. The initials stand for five key phases:

Define the problem, project goals, and customer requirements.

Measure key aspects of the current process and collect relevant data.

Analyze the data to determine the root cause of the problem.

Improve the current process by selecting and testing the best possible solutions.

Control the ongoing quality of the process by creating a standardized, monitored process with documented procedures. The goal is to identify and correct potential variations before they lead to a problem or defect.

To designate levels of expertise, Six Sigma borrows from martial arts. Individuals earn belt colors by demonstrating mastery of Six Sigma's methodology:

Yellow Belts have basic training in the methodology.

Green Belts receive enough training to work on a Six Sigma project team and lead small-scale improvement projects. They also support larger projects headed by Black Belts.

Black Belts are highly trained and adept with statistical tools. Their ability to interpret analytics helps them spot process-improvement opportunities and act as coaches to Green Belts.

Master Black Belts are experts in Six Sigma quality and help guide the strategic direction for their organization's Six Sigma program. They also mentor and train Black Belts and Green Belts.

When productivity goes off-track, use a Six Sigma technique called The 5 Whys: Once you have identified a problem, ask, "Why did this happen?" Take the response to that question and again ask, "Why did this happen?" Repeat until a clearer idea of the root cause emerges.

TOOLSET: PROJECT REVIEWS

There are four steps in the process for conducting formal project reviews: prepare the session, conduct the session, collect learning, and share the learning. The review session itself takes no more than two hours if planned properly, and the PMO and the project manager need two or three hours of session preparation time. After the session, they usually spend about one more hour on reporting. The time dedicated to these sessions needs to be included in every project plan within the organization. The project office can help the project manager with all project snapshot preparation and logistics.

- **Prepare the session:** The PMO works with the project manager to gather background information, identify one or two major project areas or subjects to discuss during the session, create an agenda, and invite session participants.

- **Conduct the session:** The project manager, using the PMO as a facilitator, reviews the purpose and themes to discuss, and sets the ground rules with the group, defining the project snapshot process.

- **Collect learning:** The facilitator probes meeting attendees for what went well, lessons learned, recommendations, and key collateral and/or intellectual material for reuse. The facilitator takes notes on key learning or material to be submitted, eliciting sufficient details from the participants so that results are reusable. The PMO summarizes key learning from the session and prepares a presentation.

- **Share the learning:** The project manager and selected members of the project team share their learning with appropriate parties. The PMO distributes outcomes to teams responsible for any elements used in the project, including solution development teams, and to people development managers.

After the session, the facilitator—that is, the PMO—collects the outcomes on a document or template and reviews the information with the project manager prior to distributing it to the team or posting it on the intranet site.

At the beginning, I (Bucero), as an experienced project manager, facilitated these sessions and trained project managers to do them. The results were very good. Participants commented, "It was a great opportunity to talk among team members and managers openly"; "To think and discuss about what happened and not about who was guilty has been great."

After many years running these sessions for customers in different countries, I get the same feedback. I find some differences in running project snapshots from country to country in Europe, based on different cultures and behaviors, but no differences have been found regarding the session results. Investing in knowledge management is key for a successful project business.

TOOLSET: RESPONSIBLE PROJECT MANAGERS

Over the years we have observed that project leaders who embrace responsibility have these characteristics in common:

- **They get the job done.** No one can do the minimum and reach his or her maximum potential. Responsible project managers have a clear idea about the effort required to accomplish the projects they manage and the impact their projects have on business success.

- **They are willing to go the extra mile.** Responsible people never protest, "That's not my job." They are willing to do whatever it takes to complete the work needed by the project or by the organization. To succeed, they are willing to put the organization ahead of their own agenda.

- **They are driven by excellence.** Excellence is a great motivator. People who desire excellence—and work hard to achieve it—are almost always responsible. Make high quality the goal, and responsibility will naturally follow. Always be ready to learn during the whole project life cycle.

- **They produce regardless of the situation.** The ultimate quality of a responsible person is the ability to finish a job. In order to lead, they have to produce and make team members produce, too.

Here are some suggestions to improve your own level of responsibility:

- **Keep hanging in there.** Sometimes an inability to deliver in difficult circumstances is due to a lack of persistence. Creative solutions may surface out of a sustained effort.

- **Admit it when results are not good enough.** If you have trouble achieving project excellence, it is possible that you have lowered your standards. Look at your personal life for places where you have let things slip, then make changes to set higher standards for yourself. This will help you reset your bar of excellence.

- **Find better tools.** If you find that your standards are high, your attitude is good, and you consistently work hard, and you still do not achieve the way you would like, get better equipped. Improve your skills by taking classes, reading books, and listening to audio resources. Find a mentor. Do whatever it takes to become better at what you do.

TOOLSET: BEING A COMPETENT PROJECT MANAGER

Competence is a key to credibility, and credibility is the key to influence others. Most team members will follow competent project managers. If you want to cultivate competence, implement these suggestions:

What To Do	How To Do It
1. Show up every day.	Project managers are usually under a lot of pressure. Stop for a few minutes every day and relax. Find time to do some physical exercise every day. Highly competent people take everything a step further. They are people that come ready to play every day, and in order to be ready you need to be present and feel good physically and mentally.
2. Keep improving.	All highly competent people continually search for ways to keep learning, growing, and improving. By focusing on project stakeholders' reactions, you can learn a lot every day. Do a retrospective analysis, at least at the end of every project. Involve your project stakeholders, listen to them, and learn and share best practices.
3. Follow through with excellence.	We have never met a person we considered competent who didn't follow through on commitments. Quality is never an accident—it is always the result of high intention, sincere effort, intelligent direction, and skillful execution; it represents the wise choice of many alternatives. Be persistent.
4. Accomplish more than expected.	Highly competent people always go the extra mile. Good enough is never good enough. They think, reflect, and move forward.
5. Inspire others.	Highly competent leaders do more than perform at a high level. They inspire and motivate their people to do the same. Competent project managers need to lead by example, giving the benefit of the doubt to their people, allowing some mistakes, and coaching them through learning experiences.

To perform as a complete project manager, improve your competence by doing the following:

- **Get your head in the game.** If you have been mentally or emotionally detached from your work, it is time to reengage.

- **Redefine the standard.** If you are not performing at a consistently high level, reexamine your standards.

- **Find three ways to improve.** Nobody keeps improving without being intentional about it. Do research to find three things you can do to improve your professional skills. Then dedicate the time and money to follow through.

TOOLSET: PROJECT SKILLS FOR EXECUTIVES

Michael O'Brochta, PMP, president of Zozer Inc. in Roanoke, Virginia, shares a list of executive actions for project management in his paper "How to Accelerate Executive Support for Projects" (2011). This is a list of what top-performing (that is, complete) project managers want and need from their executives.

What Executives Should Do	How They Should Do It
Organize and manage work as projects	Structure work into distinct projects with a designated project manager. Actively participate as a sponsor. Be accountable to the project manager. Grant authority. Establish and manage against baselines.
Pick the right projects	Clearly identify a limited number of top-priority projects. Fewer projects equate to more success and higher output. Avoid over-committing to too many projects.
Maintain close stakeholder relationships	Work with stakeholders and customers to further strengthen relationships with them. Build credibility and equity. Manage benefits.
Use a suitable project management process	Provide a project management process suitable for the type of work and the experience levels of the project managers. Advocate process tailoring for each project.
Ensure projects follow a documented plan	Require documented project plans. Provide adequate time for planning and resist pressure to cut planning short. Use a baseline plan as basis for decisions. Maintain accountability to the plan.
Ensure projects are based on requirements	Require documented project requirements. Provide adequate time for and resist pressure to shortcut requirements definition. Use baseline requirements as a basis for decisions. Maintain accountability to the requirements.
Require a basis for cost estimates	Require cost estimates to have a written, definitive basis. Include risks and management reserves. Link costs to schedule and requirements.

Ensure resources are sufficient	Ensure that adequate resources are provided; avoid shortchanging. Solicit impact assessment in response to change. Adjust resources in relation to schedule and requirements adjustments.
Engage middle management help	Ensure middle managers work to resolve conflicts, make decisions, and provide project assistance.
Behave like an executive—ask the right questions	Understand the relationship between the executive and project manager roles. Practice servant leadership. Create a culture for project success. Ask questions to engage the project manager.

Furthermore, Michael provides suggestions for how project managers can get executives to act in accordance with the list above:

What To Do	How To Do It
Use the executive actions lists	Make a list of desired executive actions for project success. Tailor the list. Use the list.
Emphasize the value of successful projects	Since the number-one reason for executive failure is bad execution, recognize the dependence of executives on projects (which are about execution).
Underscore the importance of project management	Since the new theme in new-product development is speed, recognize the dependence of executives on project management (which is about speed management).
Behave like an alpha (the top 2% of project managers)	Again, since the number-one reason for executive failure is bad execution, recognize the dependence of executives on project managers who act as if they have authority (as the top 2% of project managers do). Act like an alpha: spend twice as much time communicating and planning than a non-alpha.

Communicate using business context	Express project benefits and performance in business terms. Speak the executive's language. Reference the value of project management research.
Understand and use power	Use sources of expert power and associative sources of power to influence without authority.
Leverage sponsors and champions	Amplify your power as a project manager through relationships with sponsors and champions.
Form a project management council	Amplify your power as a project manager through relationships with project management thought leaders. Help executives implement the desired actions for project success.

ENVIRONMENT SKILLS

TOOLSET: DEVELOP A PURPOSE

In *Purpose: The Starting Point of Great Companies*, author Nikos Mourkogiannis writes, "Purpose is your moral DNA. It's what you believe without having to think." There are three reasons purpose is crucial to a firm's success:

1. Purpose is the primary source of achievement.
2. Purpose reveals the underlying dynamics of any human activity.
3. Purpose is all that successful leaders want to talk about.

Here are some key ideas from the book:

- Moral ideas determine the effectiveness of people and of intangible assets.
- Political winners tend to be those groups who can evoke a clear, consistent purpose that attracts followers.
- In contrast to purpose, codes or governance practices are not designed to make things happen but to prevent or restrain action that might lead to liabilities.
- Leaders like Thomas Watson Sr. of IBM are effective not because of personality but because of the purpose they subscribe to and communicate to colleagues.
- A leader like Henry Ford learned that thinking first of money instead of the purpose of work brings on fear of failure; this fear blocks every avenue of business.
- Heroes who eventually fail do so by outliving their purpose.
- Good morale happens when supported by four building blocks—rewards, tasks, community, and purpose.
- The combination of energy and a strong sense of purpose creates a sense of direction.
- Shared understandings are vital.

- Purpose creates even longer-lasting and enduring advantage than strategic positioning.

- Leaders have to manage purpose and strategy so that they are aligned; when they drift apart, the organization starts to follow two masters ... and is unlikely to satisfy either fully.

- Linking rewards to purpose sends signals that the company is serious about fulfilling its purpose.

- People who create great organizations choose a form of purpose along the lines of:
  - Discovery (love of the new)
  - Excellence (purpose of the intrinsically beautiful and elegant)
  - Altruism (urge to increase happiness) or
  - Heroism (drive to achieve).

To illustrate the forms of purpose, consider four main characters from the movie *Pirates of the Caribbean*. Which character do you most closely relate to? The pirate Jack Sparrow is an adventurer, driven by *discovery*. His partner and foil, the blacksmith Will Turner, is an avatar of *excellence*, holding to both craft and moral standards. The governor's daughter, Elizabeth Swann, is *altruistic*, pursuing the greater good for everyone. The mutineer Captain Barbossa represents *heroism* in seeking a treasure no mortal man was meant to have. How each of us relates to these characters provides clues about our own purpose. Be true to this purpose and make it clear to others as a personal statement of your leadership values.

Our challenge to each wannabe complete project manager is this: can you clearly state your personal, project, and organizational purpose? If not, you have a call to action. If so, you are on the path to success. Purpose is a force that sustains you throughout chaos.

TOOLSET: FORCE FIELD ANALYSIS

Table 5-1 explains the process of preparing a force field analysis. See Figure 5-1 for an illustration of a force field analysis model.

TABLE 5-1: How to Prepare a Force Field Analysis

What To Do	How To Do It
Summarize the change	Summarize the change that is being evaluated in one phrase and write that phrase in the middle of the page. You may want to highlight it with a rectangular border.
Brainstorm	Using brainstorming and interview techniques, make a list of forces that are driving the intended change and a list of those resisting the change. Include factors such as time, money, use of human resources, customer satisfaction, employee satisfaction, and sustainability.
List the driving forces	List the driving forces vertically, along with an estimate of their strength on a scale from 1 to +10.
List the forces against the change	List the forces against the change—the restraining forces—vertically, along with an estimate of their strength on a scale from 1 to –10.
Add up the strength ratings	At the bottom of the page, add up the strength ratings for the driving forces. Do the same for the resisting forces.
Look at the result	If the driving forces are substantially higher, the climate is definitely appropriate for change. If the numbers are close or the resisting forces are higher, determine which driving forces can be strengthened and which resisting forces can be countered.
Create a plan	Any change in any force causes the status quo (equilibrium) point to shift. Create a plan to strengthen the driving forces and weaken the resisting forces. Include nudges as well as large changes in the force vectors across the chart.

Re-create the force field analysis diagram	Once you have implemented the plan, re-create the force field analysis diagram with updated information and evaluate it as before.
Repeat the previous two steps	Repeat the previous two steps until the strength of the forces for change exceeds the strength of the forces against change. Once this is the case, you are ready to proceed with your change initiative.

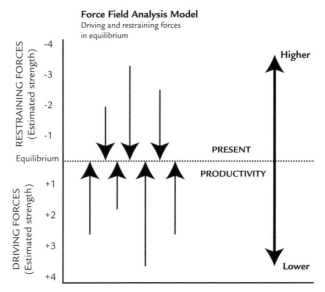

FIGURE 5-1: Force Field Analysis Model

TOOLSET: STRENGTHEN PROJECT MANAGER CREDIBILITY

Pay attention to:

Sharpness: Clarify your commitment, needs, interests, values, vision, and project objectives. Encourage all managers and team members to understand these same qualities. Train them to ask questions of various project stakeholders.

Harmony: Communicate goals, direction, and the principles that guide your actions. Harmony exists when team members widely share, support, and endorse the intent of a commonly understood set of aims and aspirations.

Passion: Encourage yourself and others to act on strongly felt values. Passion exists when principles are taken seriously; when they reflect deep feelings, standards, and emotional bonds; and when they are the basis of critical organizational resource allocations.

Exploring yourself: Look into the mirror and ask yourself questions like: Who are you? What do you believe in? What do you stand for? Once clear on your own values, translate them into a set of guiding principles that you communicate to the team you want to lead.

Sensitivity to others: Leadership implies a relationship, and you will only be able to build that relationship on mutual understanding and respect. Team members believe in their leaders when they believe the leaders have their best interests at heart.

Confirming shared values: Confirm a core of shared values passionately and speak enthusiastically on behalf of the project.

Developing capacity: Project managers need to develop the capacity of their team members to keep their commitments. Ensure that educational opportunities exist for individuals to build their knowledge and skill.

Serving a purpose: Leadership is a service provided to the team, on behalf of the organization.

Sustaining hope: Teams need a positive attitude in troubling times of transition. People with high hopes also are high achievers. Project team members expect their leaders to have the courage of their convictions and to stand up for their beliefs. Realize that, day by day, the best way to build credibility on your project is to "walk the talk."

TOOLSET: ENVIRONMENTAL ASSESSMENT SURVEY INSTRUMENT (EASI)

The purpose of an EASI is to measure how well the environment supports project management in an organization. Each of the ten components assessed relates to a chapter in *Creating an Environment for Successful Projects* (2004).

The following questions refer to your current project. If you are not now working on a project, or if your current project has just begun and you feel you cannot answer the questions accurately, then refer to the last project you worked on when answering these questions. If you are an upper manager, think of the project or projects with which you are most closely associated.

Rate the truth of each statement on a scale of 1 to 7. Use the following guidelines:

1 means the statement is true to an extremely small extent, never or not at all.
4 means it is true to an average extent, or about normal in degree or frequency.
7 means it is true to an extremely large extent, always or without fail.

A benchmark report is available from englundr@englundpmc.com that shows cumulative averages and a percentile chart from thousands of people worldwide who have completed this survey.

1. Project-Based Organization

1. Projects are important for the future of this organization.
2. Upper managers appreciate the role of project management.
3. The current organizational structure supports project work.
4. People in this organization embrace teams, consensus action, empowerment, trust, and open communication.
5. The organization adapts readily to change.
6. Managers are authentic and act with integrity.
7. Upper managers work together as a team.
8. Everyone acts with concern for the success of the project.
9. Success in the organization depends on the performance of all participants.
10. Clear measures are in place for project success.

_____ **Total: Project-Based Organization: Average** _____

2. **Strategic Emphasis**

1. I am aware of my organization's business strategy.
2. The project goal is clearly linked to a business strategic goal.
3. Team members understand how this project adds value to the organization.
4. Core team members participated in defining the project goal statement.
5. Consistent criteria were applied to select this project.
6. I know how this project links with other projects to implement organizational strategy.
7. This project was selected based on a comparative priority ranking of contribution to organizational strategy.
8. The team trusts upper management that this project is not likely to be canceled unless there is a change in strategy.
9. The project has a clearly defined, supportive upper management sponsor.
10. I can focus on this project without disruption from other projects.

_____ **Total: Strategic Emphasis: Average** _____

3. **Upper Management Support**

1. Managers of all team members fully support the need for this project.
2. Upper managers allow the team to do the job without interference.
3. Upper managers do not change project specifications.
4. The project deadline was negotiated with the project sponsor.
5. Upper managers understand the benefits of project management.
6. The sponsor works with the project manager to negotiate any changes in schedule or resource levels.
7. Organizational reward systems properly motivate work on projects.
8. Upper managers are more interested in project results than they are in controlling the project.
9. I feel that upper managers fully understand the PM process.
10. Upper managers support the project planning process.

_____ **Total: Upper Management Support: Average** _____

4. Project Team Support

1. (Most) project team members work full time on this project.
2. A core team has been established to work together from the beginning to the end of the project.
3. Project core team members are located together when they work on this project.
4. Project team members do not feel they are working on too many projects.
5. Teamwork is rewarded in this organization.
6. A customer or end user representative is on the core team.
7. Project team members want to be on this team.
8. Upper managers provide support for project startup activities.
9. Upper managers do not interchange or pull people off projects.
10. All project team members feel responsible for project success.

_____ **Total: Project Team Support: Average** _____

5. Organization Support

1. Projects align with meeting the needs of customers.
2. Project priorities are consistent across the organization.
3. The organization rewards team members if they are successful on this project.
4. A consistent project management process or methodology is used.
5. Balance exists between the needs of projects and the needs of continuing operations within the organization.
6. The project manager position has the necessary scope and sufficient authority for the project size.
7. The organization supports desired behaviors with structure, measures, and rewards.
8. Projects integrate well across the organization.
9. Organizational structure supports rather than creates obstacles to project work.
10. The organization is flexible enough to accommodate project requirements.

_____ **Total: Organization Support: Average** _____

6. Project Management Information Systems

1. The benefits of good communications are apparent to all stakeholders.
2. The project plan has been communicated to all project stakeholders.
3. Sharing information about this project reduces anxiety in the organization.
4. Team members are aware of deadlines for their activities.
5. Project team members communicate easily with each other.
6. People speak the truth to upper managers without fear of recrimination.
7. Communication and political plans are developed, used, and updated throughout the project.
8. Available information about the project answers stakeholder questions, is there when they need it, and is easy to understand.
9. The information system supports organizational learning.
10. Reports are streamlined and provide the basis for making decisions and taking appropriate actions.

_____ Total: **Project Management Information Systems: Average** _____

7. Project Manager Selection and Development

1. This project has a single project manager appointed.
2. The project manager was selected based on a formal process.
3. Criteria for selection were based on ability to do the job, not as a reward for past work.
4. The project manager is enthusiastic about this project and managing it.
5. A curriculum is available that provides training on the necessary technical, behavioral, organizational, and business skills.
6. The project manager receives adequate training.
7. Project managers have the opportunity to network with other PMs and share best practices.
8. The organization has identified competencies and skills for project managers at different levels based upon project complexity.
9. The manager of this project has a clear development plan, or career path, to follow.
10. _Project manager_ is a recognized job title in this organization.

_____ Total: **Project Manager Selection and Development: Average** _____

8. Learning Organization

1. People on the project and across the organization believe that continuous learning is a priority.
2. Experimentation and creativity are encouraged.
3. Upper managers survey and act on employee feedback.
4. Decisions and action are based upon data and evidence available from a project management information system.
5. Project goals are balanced among performance, experience, and learning.
6. Upper managers encourage learning from mistakes as well as from successes.
7. A project review will be held at the end of this project.
8. Outcomes from the project review help improve the project management process.
9. The results of the project review will be shared with other teams across the organization.
10. Management will take action on key findings from the project review.

_____ **Total: Learning Organization: Average** _____

9. Project Office

1. There is a person or group in charge of improving project management in this organization.
2. Resources are available to assist in starting or implementing stages in the project life cycle.
3. A project management methodology provides common terminology and consistent expectations for managing this project.
4. I know where to get project management training.
5. Consulting and facilitation assistance are available within the organization.
6. The project is listed on a master plan.
7. Administrative support is available for this project.
8. A central repository exists to capture and extract information on best practices.
9. I can access a mediator to resolve cross-project or cross-organizational issues.
10. A project office is available to help select, execute, and close my project.

_____ **Total: Project Office: Average** _____

10. Project Management Culture

1. We have an inventory of all projects underway and proposed.
2. Management support for project work exists at all levels of the organization.
3. Project selection is a clear-cut process.
4. Upper managers model the desired behavior for project teams.
5. Recruiting "accidental project managers" is not the normal staffing process for projects.
6. Project management is viewed as a career position.
7. Reviews are conducted for all projects and shared with other project teams.
8. We function in a trusting, open environment.
9. Management values authentic behavior—saying what you believe.
10. We practice integrity in all interactions—doing what we said.

_____**Total: Project Management Culture: Average** _____

©Englund Project Management Consultancy, www.englundpmc.com

TOOLSET: USING AN ACTION PLAN TEMPLATE TO CREATE AN ENVIRONMENT FOR MORE SUCCESSFUL PROJECTS

Creating an Environment for Successful Projects
Action Plan Template

Name: _____ I AM _____

Organization: _____ Where I Work _____

Date: _____ The President _____

Project-Based Organization   score _____   benchmark _____

• Emphasis: ☐ more   ☐ less   ☒ OK

Steps:

• Identify a core management team to sponsor a project management initiative

• Begin a public relations campaign to highlight the importance of projects and how we need to revitalize our approach in order to accomplish our mission

• Ask people on my teams to take accountability for overall success of each project—explain what this means and how behaviors can change

---

Strategic Emphasis   score _____   benchmark _____

• Emphasis: ☒ more   ☐ less   ☐ OK

Steps:

• Ask functional manager and staff to clarify organizational strategy with priorities for this next year

• Convene a guiding coalition to establish categories with attendant criteria for selecting projects in each category in order to meet larger goals

• Implement a simple portfolio management process immediately and work with other managers to develop a system to support it over the next 18 months

• Develop a sponsorship training overview and assign a sponsor to each project

Upper Management Support   score _____   benchmark _____
- Emphasis: [x] more   [ ] less   [ ] OK

Steps:
- Bring in a consultant to get the attention of upper managers about their role to better support project-based work
- Begin negotiating deadlines for each goal and task
- Set priorities with managers and engage in dialogue about what to delay when something new gets added
- Ask team members what rewards they prefer

Project Team Support   score _____   benchmark _____
- Emphasis: [x] more   [ ] less   [ ] OK

Steps:
- Negotiate better commitments for people's time on projects
- Formalize project startup events for each project—make sure sponsor is present
- Engage team in dialogue about purpose, vision, and mission statements
- Bring in customer occasionally to share needs, review progress, and give feedback

Organization Support   score _____   benchmark _____
- Emphasis: [ ] more   [ ] less   [x] OK

Steps:
- Standardize a project management methodology so we use common terminology and set consistent expectations across projects
- Suggest the core management team put a master list of projects together with time line; coordinate this list across the organization
- Pilot a project-centric suborganization on the org chart for one or two key projects

PM Information Systems   score _____   benchmark _____
- Emphasis: [x] more   [ ] less   [ ] OK

Steps:
- Take more time to establish rapport and improve the environment for open communications
- Urge people to share ALL news (good and bad); provide constructive feedback when they do
- Set up a project web page and a place for all team members to share comments
- Ask key stakeholders what information they need and how they use it
- Shorten the monthly status report and provide a more potent executive summary

PM Selection and Development   score _____   benchmark _____
- Emphasis: [x] more   [ ] less   [ ] OK

Steps:
- Begin culling PM selection process to get people enthusiastic and piqued to manage projects
- Get agreement with other managers about PM and team competencies that best fit this organization
- Encourage PMs to take internal courseware as well as participate in outside activities
- Set up monthly lunches for PMs to get together and informally share lessons learned and concerns and learn new topics

Learning Organization   score _____   benchmark _____
- Emphasis: [x] more   [ ] less   [ ] OK

Steps:
- Set up objectives for each project about desired performance, experiences, and learning
- More systematically list, prioritize, and act upon lessons learned from each project
- Begin each project by reviewing past project reviews and presenting to the team and management what should be done the same and what done differently on this project
- Change own attitude (and eventually others') towards failures—these are opportunities to learn and improve, not berate ourselves or sweep under the carpet

Project Office   score _____   benchmark _____
- Emphasis: [ ] more   [x] less   [ ] OK

Steps:
- Act as a project office of one, until such time as the organization is ready to standardize the process more and establish a formal project office
- Plant seeds and start building a guiding coalition and harnessing internal support for a full-service project office

Project Management Culture   score _____   benchmark _____
- Emphasis: ☐ more   ☐ less   ☒ OK

Steps:
- Apply all the previous steps to help improve our relatively weak project management culture
- Demonstrate trustworthy behavior every day and in every way
- Be a model of authentic leadership and act with integrity
- Call others to task (carefully!) when commitments are violated

Notes:
I'm inspired to think more systemically about these issues!

TOOLSET: ENVIRONMENTAL ANALYSIS—SWOT

As with any profession, there are project management tools of the trade. One of the helpful niche tools complete project managers can use is SWOT, an assessment of strengths, weaknesses, opportunities, and threats. Bruce Woerner, PMP, Certified Six Sigma Black Belt, provides a summary of this tool:

How It Works

SWOT is a tool I used in the consulting world, and I was reminded of it again when I went through Six Sigma Black Belt training. Essentially, SWOT is a diagnostic analysis used to assess a situation.

It is a "point in time" measurement to determine current state and chart a path forward. It is particularly helpful in situations where there is competition, political challenge, stakeholder resistance, and other potential roadblocks. It can be used as both a strategic and operational tool.

SWOT can be visualized in a grid.

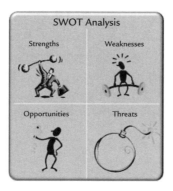

When to Use It

1. Triggered SWOT

SWOT usage can be triggered by the risk management process. Certain risks or changes may be of a broad nature, and standard risk management may be insufficient. These situations call for the need for a SWOT analysis.

Examples of risks that may trigger the use of a SWOT analysis:
- Key stakeholder change
- Funding change
- Political climate changes
- Regulatory environment changes

- Poor-quality deliverables
- Key vendor having solvency issues
- Competitor delivers a similar product in the middle of the development cycle.

2. Scheduled SWOT

In addition to triggered SWOT, this tool can be used on a periodic basis. In my experience, a SWOT should be done quarterly on high-profile projects and semiannually on lower-risk projects. Since SWOT is a tool used to do a "step back" analysis, using it too often will not reap additional benefits.

SWOT Process

Whether scheduled or triggered, here is the process to follow:

1. Start with the project charter and assess the current state to complete the areas in the grid above. Each area gets its own page. Use brainstorming to start, and ask these types of questions:
   a) Strengths
      - What are the scope, objectives, and critical success factors?
      - How is this project delivering on those?
      - What unique and compelling skills does the project team bring to the project?
   b) Opportunities
      - Are there untapped areas to extend the project impact?
      - Can current project success be extended? How so?
      - Are there unique skills or resources that the project team has to ensure project success?
      - Does the project have stakeholders acting as advocates for project success?
   c) Weaknesses
      - What weaknesses does the project team have in their ability to deliver upon the stated scope, objectives, and critical success factors?
      - Review the risk log—are there high-level risks that endanger the success of the project?
   d) Threats
      - Ask yourself and key stakeholders: what keeps them up at night with regard to the project? Ask for the top item.
      - Review the cost structure and political landscape. An example of a political threat might be the loss of the project champion.
      - Are there changes in the political or regulatory environment?

- Are there things outside the project that could make the mission obsolete?

2. Once the current state is known and documented, assess each area for potential future state following the same grid structure.

3. Perform a gap analysis between current and future state and determine what needs to change.

4. Prepare a summary SWOT with a single page each for Current State SWOT, Improved Future State SWOT, and Gap Analysis. Using these pages as the foundation, add a summary about what needs to be done in response to the SWOT. The typical outcome is a bulleted list with owners and specific roles and responsibilities.

5. Vet solution with team, trusted advisors, and key stakeholders. Based on the feedback, the SWOT can be adjusted.

6. Refresh the SWOT analysis periodically throughout the project.

7. Use SWOT as one of multiple inputs into lessons learned at project closure.

Conclusion

A practical outcome of a SWOT is something actionable that improves the project's probability of success. SWOT is a simple and practical tool to allow the complete project manager to think strategically about elements in the environment and react for the betterment of the project.

TOOLSET: EXTREME PROJECT MANAGEMENT

Depending on the environment, extreme project management may be an alternative to traditional project management. (Complete project managers keep all possibilities in their toolsets.)

Doug DeCarlo, principal of The Doug DeCarlo Group, defines an extreme project as

> a complex, high-change, high-stress, self-correcting venture in search of a desired result.
>
> The main difference between a traditional project and an extreme project has to do with the level of predictability surrounding the undertaking. Extreme projects live in turbulent environments: high speed, high change and high uncertainty. Requirements are constantly changing throughout the project in response to internal and external environmental factors that include competition, technology, shifts in customer needs, regulatory requirements, and/or economic conditions. Change is the norm. Change is the project.
>
> Fundamental to success on an extreme project is to apply the appropriate method and mindset. Mindset is one's own mental conditioning and emotional programming.

Self-Diagnostic Tool

DeCarlo's tool, below, can help you determine whether you have the right mindset to successfully run an extreme project.

Newtonian Mindset	Quantum Mindset
Stability is the norm	Chaos is the norm
The world is linear and predictable	Uncertainty reigns
The world is controllable	Murphy's law rules
Minimize change	Welcome change
Increase the feeling of security by adding rigor to the process	Increase the feeling of security by relaxing controls

Newtonian Hat	Quantum Hat
Deliver on the planned result	Discover the desired result
Use the plan to drive results	Use results to drive planning
Aim, aim, fire	Fire, then redirect the bullet
Establish stronger procedures and policies	Agree on guidelines, principles, and values
Keep tight control on the process	Keep the process flexible
Correct to the baseline	Correct to what's possible
Be a taskmaster	Be a relationship manager
Get it right the first time	Get it right the last time

If your default settings are at odds with the world around you, you are most likely suffering from Newtonian Neurosis—the ego-based compulsive need to bludgeon the world to conform to your project plan. The fact that the project plan was fiction in the first place does not seem to deter the Newtonian Neurotic who finds him- or herself in the unenviable position of trying to retrofit reality to agree with fiction. The Quantum mindset and hat represent the more compatible temperament and management style for running an extreme project (2001).

TOOLSET: ENVIRONMENT FOR TRAINING

Training is integral to the development of complete project managers. How to get that training in cost- and content-effective ways, especially in challenging economic times, engenders much debate and angst. We (Englund and Bucero) are long experienced in developing and delivering in-person courses. The interaction and sharing that occurs is priceless. Technology is now offering ways to achieve these values across time and space.

We asked Stefano M. Stefan, Ph.D., director of online program development at the University of California, Irvine Extension, to share his approach to fostering student engagement and interactivity in distance learning:

> One of the challenges in distance education is how to create an environment in which students and instructors can engage each other online in the same way they can engage each other in a traditional classroom setting. This is closely related to another challenge, namely how an instructor can be perceived by students as being an important contributor to a course beyond simply being identified as the originator of the course content. The latter challenge has important implications in the perceived value of the course.
>
> We are by no means unique in our approach at UC Irvine Extension. We host our online courses on Moodle (Modular Object-Oriented Dynamic Learning Environment), a widely-used open-source learning management system that includes numerous features that allow students and instructors to interact either in real time or asynchronously. Before delving into several of these features, let me briefly describe a "typical" online course offering.
>
> The target audience consists primarily of working professionals in a variety of fields ranging from project management to software engineering. Students often work late, have a busy schedule that includes business travel, and wish to avoid driving to class on congested freeways. They seek relevant, no-nonsense education or training that they can apply on the job, immediately. Hence, distance learning becomes increasingly attractive.
>
> Instructors are industry professionals who have well-defined areas of expertise. For example, when taking a course on financial management, the instructor is a financial manager. Instructors bring their own personal experience and subject matter knowledge to the classroom, which complements "theoretical" knowledge found in textbooks.
>
> Students learn through three primary avenues:
>
> 1. What the instructor teaches them directly
> 2. What they learn from textbooks, journal articles, websites, published case studies, and other preexisting materials

3. What they learn from each other by working on projects and assignments, and by participating in online discussions

So, how do we do all this online?

First, instructors prepare presentations in advance and post them on Moodle so their students can view them later at their leisure. These presentations correspond to live classroom lectures. Three modalities can be offered:

1. Recorded, narrated presentations that use PowerPoint (or similar presentation software) or that demonstrate software applications.
2. Written documents including diagrams, photographs, and other graphical elements. Instead of listening to the instructor speaking, students read what the instructor has written.
3. Live sessions (*synchronous* sessions) using an online conferencing tool such as WebEx, in which students log in and/or dial in for the audio portion simultaneously.

While most instructors use only one modality for their entire course, a few use more than one. In fact, we encourage this, since it makes things more interesting for the students. It's not unusual for an instructor to supplement his or her asynchronous course with periodic live WebEx sessions for office hours or general discussions. Most instructors are familiar with PowerPoint, and many use it frequently while teaching in the classroom. It's not very difficult to extrapolate from lecturing in front of a live audience to lecturing in front of a computer screen with recording software running. In fact, without the distractions of a live audience, recorded presentations are often more concise and shorter while conveying the same amount of content.

The use of textbooks, journal articles, websites, etc., is essentially the same whether the course is online or in a classroom. Of course, students at a distance do not have the luxury of visiting the campus bookstore to purchase textbooks and supplementary materials, but today anything that might be purchased in a physical store can be purchased online. Sitting at home reading from the textbook and completing a homework assignment looks the same whether the course is online or on-ground.

With regard to online interactivity, most online learning management systems feature discussion forums, which allow the instructor to post a question or "discussion-starting" prompt to which students must post responses. Students can also comment on each other's posts, thereby generating a written back-and-forth "conversation" that is in many ways similar to an in-class discussion (though it may last several days as students log in and out at different times).

A good discussion forum prompt sparks conversation. It *doesn't* ask a question with a definite "correct" or "incorrect" answer; it *does* ask a question to which different students might have *different* responses. Sometimes the question might be slightly controversial, thereby eliciting a variety of opinions, or it might ask students to discuss their own personal experience.

As an example from the world of project management, a question about the elements of the triple constraint probably would not spark much controversy or deep discussion. However, a question that asks students to describe how effective (or ineffective) project management practices are in their own companies is much more interesting and engenders responses that are more diverse.

In the realm of software engineering, typically the code runs or it doesn't! Nevertheless, there are marvelous opportunities for useful discussions–such as the pros and cons of outsourcing application development overseas or the challenges of developing code when working as part of a team of developers who are scattered around the globe. At the very least, discussion forums are places where students ask questions and the instructor, in answering those questions, provides some "extra" teaching.

In addition to discussion forums, Moodle has a chat feature in which instructors and students can interact in real time and, of course, WebEx or similar products used to supplement Moodle offer obvious opportunities for live interactivity. Other ways to foster interactivity and collaboration include such capabilities as Internet telephony (such as Skype) and online document sharing (such as Google Docs).

Thus, the instructor not only has to prepare content for teaching but also must create a *social context* for interactive learning by setting up forums and chat rooms and by orchestrating student activities to take advantage of those capabilities. An instructor who does this and actively participates in online activities cannot but help being visible to the students. This is the perceived value of the course. The content that the instructor imparts to the students is not worth very much by itself. Anyone can find plenty of free information on the Internet or can spend a few dollars to purchase textbooks. What makes an online course truly valuable and worth the fee is everything else the instructor adds to it in terms of *facilitation*.

Much of the discussion or even controversy surrounding distance education stems from the question of whether an online course is "as good as" or whether it can "replace" a traditional classroom-based course. This is not really a very useful discussion! It is clear that online education is as effective as classroom-based education (U.S. Department of Education 2010) and that it is a viable option for working adults. What we need to be discussing is how to make online courses even better–with well-designed, interactive content and instructors who take the time to engage their students online.

The instructor training program at UC Irvine Extension focuses heavily on facilitation and on making courses "inviting" to students. No learning management system is perfect, so we rely on instructors to add a top layer of instructional design that draws students into the course and leads them through the learning experience. One of the first things that students see when they enter a course is a welcome message from the instructor in a discussion forum. They can then respond and introduce themselves. We encourage students to post photos of themselves, as well, in order to enhance a sense of cohesiveness.

Distance learning will not replace classroom-based instruction, nor can it pretend to do so. However, the online environment can foster a strong sense of social cohesion just as gathering in a classroom can. What's more, the concept of an online social environment is becoming increasingly familiar, especially to users of social media (Facebook, Twitter, etc.). In the near future, people will recognize distance learning as complementing classroom-based instruction just as social media is complementing face-to-face socializing.

As an instructor in Stefano's program, I (Englund) can attest that distance learning is both content and cost effective. I have taught many online sessions of Management, Leadership, and Team Building in a Project Environment and now Creating the Project Office. Students probably get even more involved than in-person sessions; they submit written essays every week online, and they read and comment on classmate essays. In a classroom, a student may be passive and resist speaking up; with distance learning, they have to communicate, in writing, or they will not get credit for the course. Online education provides ample practice for operating in virtual teams.

Course review postings by students reveal high satisfaction with the pace, convenience, storytelling approach to sharing experiences, and changed thinking that occurs through distance learning. Here is an example:

Comment on the process you went through and any insights gained in preparing and writing your leadership effectiveness essay. Also comment on what you gained from reading other participant essays. How effective is this form of storytelling?

When I did my essay on leadership effectiveness, I really felt good thinking and writing about my favorite boss. She wasn't my buddy, but she made me feel motivated to be my best. While I was also writing about her leadership qualities and traits, I saw some weaknesses in my leadership style because I was actually comparing my own style with my favorite leader's style and saw where I fell short of it. I am striving to be a leader who has the same soft skills, hard skills, and good PM skills as my favorite leader.

It is a joy to read my classmate forum postings. They are all insightful. I enjoyed it because I can live through their varied experiences and sometime put myself in their shoes. I am fortunate that I have classmates from diverse backgrounds (personalities, experiences, corporate industry, etc.). This class has been enriching. I could not have gained this learning by just reading books. Thanks for all the storytelling! Through the stories I read, this fills in the gap of knowledge I obtained from reading theory.

ORGANIZATION SKILLS

Faucet maker Moen Incorporated, together with Iconoculture, a leading cultural trend research firm, gathered information defining characteristics in determining consumers' level of interest in green products (*Examiner* 2009). It is possible to take their results and extend them to project organizations, allowing complete project managers to assess where they and their stakeholders position themselves with regard to creating green working organizations.

Follow along to determine which shade of green you are.

Identity	In the Larger World	In Organizations
Dark Green	Being the most eco-conscious of the four groups, Dark Greens are motivated by a sense of responsibility to the planet. They come from all age groups and tend to be from mid- to upper-economic levels. Key values for this group include a belief in the green movement, a strong sense of community, and personal pride.	We believe Dark Green project stakeholders are the most enlightened with regard to appreciating the value and contribution of project management. They have confidence in themselves and place emphasis on personal motivation, team development, and organizational social responsibility. They exude a strong sense of values and take advantage of every teaching moment to inculcate those values across the organization.

Medium Green	Medium Greens have a heightened consciousness of green issues and an interest in going green. An example would be young parents concerned about protecting the earth for their children and grandchildren, as well as protecting their families from toxins and other chemicals. They assess value against price points and are motivated by products that make it easy for them to go green. Key values for this group include hope, convenience, and prevention.	We believe Medium Green project stakeholders have seen the light about the value of project management and are anxious to explore the possibilities. They are willing to experiment, but they are also constantly aware of business implications and the need to make sound business decisions. They want processes to be simple, are fairly risk averse, and tend to balance short- versus long-term planning efforts.
Light Green	"Green is the new cool" is the motto of the Light Green group. Many embrace the eco-friendly movement because it is trendy and they desire the status associated with green's chic factor. Pricing is a critical factor in determining whether they buy green products. Key values for this group include thrift, practicality, self-expression, and status.	We believe Light Green project stakeholders are the twenty-somethings or emerging middle class who come to the table with energy and enthusiasm to make a difference or do things differently. They are eager to advance in the organization. Their budgets are limited, but they are willing to allocate resources on high-visibility projects. If project management gets them what they want, they will embrace it, or they will go after Six Sigma or Balanced Scorecard, or ....[fill in with current trend].

| **Non-Green** | These individuals are not necessarily interested in the green movement—yet. They are newly affluent or income challenged, and tend to focus on green if it brings material gain and/or survival benefits and carries the lowest cost. Key values for this group include stability, security, choice, and entitlement. | We believe Non-Green project stakeholders have been focused on their tasks or careers without much thought or interest in project management. They are pragmatic and skeptical of change or new processes. The status quo is usually fine, or else they do not get involved in efforts to work with other people to fix problems. In terms of relationships, they prize separateness rather than connection. |

Takeaways

- Recognize toxic elements that detract from organizational performance.
- Identify green elements that engage people and encourage them to use their innate talents.
- Take the initiative to apply your talents, even when the environment is not ideal.
- Engage in a relentless pursuit of leading practices—and of people who can apply them.
- Regularly assess yourself and others about your attitude and aptitude to embrace "green" environments.
- Recognize that some people are not yet willing to support a project environment that requires changing current practices.
- Be persistent in developing improved working conditions.

TOOLSET: ORGANIZATIONAL CULTURE ASSESSMENT

The following items reflect the key elements of risk assessment. Each element can be scored from 1 to 5, with a 5 indicating a strong positive response to the statement, and a 1 indicating a strong negative response.

SURVEY

1. Motivation for the Project   SCORE

1.1 There is a convincing business need for the project. _____

1.2 There are significant risks to the business if the project is unsuccessful. _____

1.3 The level of dissatisfaction with the current situation is mutually shared by employees and management. _____

1.4. Everyone feels a sense of urgency to change. _____

1.5 The extent of the impact on those affected by the project is minimal (work habits, power, security). _____

Total _____

2. Commitment to the Project

2.1 There is publicly committed sponsorship for the change. _____

2.2 Resources, time, and money are committed to sustain the change. _____

2.3 The sponsor is at a high enough level in the organization to have decision-making authority. _____

2.4 Those implementing the change are considered credible by those affected by the change. _____

2.5 The sponsor clearly understands his or her responsibility, especially when there is conflict. _____

2.6 There is a guiding coalition (other leaders supporting the sponsor) to drive the project. _____

2.7 First-line managers actively support the change. _____

Total _____

3. Shared Vision of the Project

3.1 There is a tight link between the vision for the project and the organization's overall vision. _____

3.2 People can relate the vision for the change to themselves personally, in a positive way. _____

3.3 There is a well-articulated vision of the change that is commonly understood and shared by all stakeholders. _____

3.4 There is strong leadership to sustain the vision for the change. _____

3.5 The vision statement is clear, convincing, and compelling. _____

Total _____

4. Cultural Match with the Project

4.1 The project aligns with the culture of the organization. _____

4.2 The implementation approach is appropriate to the organizational culture. _____

4.3 The strength of the culture is likely to reinforce the change direction. _____

4.4 Previous changes have been handled well in this organization. _____

4.5 Decision-making is timely and implemented. _____

4.6 There is a high degree of trust between managers and employees in the areas affected by the change. _____

Total _____

5. Organizational Alignment

5.1 Planning cycles support project resource requirements. _____

5.2 Reward structures encourage adoption of the change by all affected. _____

5.3 Processes support the sustainability of the change. _____

5.4 Consequences are articulated and followed through. _____

5.5 Management practices and behavior support the change. _____

5.6 There is a manageable level of stress in the organization. _____

Total _____

6. Communication

6.1 The organization uses three-way communication.   _____

6.2 Communication generally reaches and is understood at all levels.   _____

6.3 The communication plan is comprehensive and timely.   _____

6.4 There are different mediums for communicating in this organization.   _____

6.5 The magnitude of the change is small, both vertical and horizontally.   _____

Total   _____

7. Transition Planning

7.1 There is a transition plan in place which allows adequate time for the change.   _____

7.2 The transition plan is comprehensive, covering human, process, and technical dimensions.   _____

7.3 Transition measures are incorporated into the plan.   _____

7.4 Potential problems and risks have been identified, and there are plans for resolving them quickly.   _____

7.5 The implementation approach is aligned with the scope of the change (time frames, methods, degree of involvement).   _____

Total   _____

8. Skills

8.1 The change agents have sound skills in implementing the change process.   _____

8.2 Those affected by the change have the technical/job skills necessary to perform the new activities.   _____

8.3 People understand their personal transitioning process.   _____

8.4 There are suitable mentors available to assist people through the change.   _____

8.5 Employees have a sense of empowerment that is appropriate to the nature of the change.   _____

8.6 Teamwork is highly developed in this organization.   _____

Total   _____

Scoring Instructions

1. Total the scores for each of the eight sections.
2. Divide the section scores by the factor identified in the scoring table below to create an adjusted score.

Section	Score	Divider	Adjusted Score
Motivation		5	
Commitment		7	
Shared vision		5	
Culture		6	
Alignment		6	
Communication		5	
Planning		5	
Skills		6	

3. Total of adjusted scores   _____
4. Multiply the total adjusted score by 2.5 to create a Risk Assessment Score _____
5. Mark one of the scoring ranges below to indicate the Risk Assessment Score for the project.

Overall Risk Assessment: High (20–40) ___ Caution (41–70) ___ Low (71–100) ___

TOOLSET: IRRATIONAL PORTFOLIO MANAGEMENT

Paul O'Connor, founder and managing director of The Adept Group in Florida, influences and guides the product development and innovation efforts of clients in both consumer and industrial markets around the globe. He has conducted successful assignments, implementation initiatives, workshops, and benchmarking activities with major firms doing new product development (NPD). We share some of Paul's writings (2011) about how to approach a major issue around project portfolio management.

Perhaps you've seen it before. You are sitting in a portfolio review meeting, everybody is serious, and then the charts start appearing. At first there is not a sound. Everyone is studying what the bubbles mean. Then, as each person catches on, eyes start shifting back and forth at each other. A few murmurs are heard as the thought waves get sent out. "Does the VP at the head of the table really believe these numbers?" "What was the project team smoking when they offered up that revenue amount?"

Some people may be thinking whether the management team can make decisions based on the numbers. And then they do. Management makes a decision to shift projects around, all based on crappy numbers! How did they do it? There is nothing rational here!

We have irrational numbers feeding normal irrational decision-making!

On the issue of trying to manage the portfolio with poor data quality and the actions needed to improve data quality, people express the difficulty of asking a project manager or a project team to go back and change valuations and risk numbers on their projects, just because some project management office or portfolio manager finds the numbers questionable. While we know that good portfolio management decisions require good numbers and analytical support, should the portfolio manager actually get involved in improving the quality of the decision-making? Undoubtedly, the answer is yes! But first, let me share an understanding of how the decisions get made when there is murky or uncertain data.

To do this, we need to dive into the topic of microeconomics. There are two branches of microeconomics that pull at each other in the quest to make economic sense of things. One branch supports rational, analytical thinking, while the other supports behavioral (psychology-influenced) thinking. There is much debate between the two branches as to which is more correct in interpreting the world of economic decisions. Suffice it to say, though, both clearly have demonstrated meaningful contributions.

On the rational, analytic side we see foundational building blocks such as supply vs. demand, comparative net present values, and efficient frontiers. Basically, the rational side says, "Show me the numbers, and then I will decide the best course forward."

The behavioral side is a bit different. It turns out that when things look too complex or uncertain, our inner [TV cartoon character] Homer Simpson can take over (see Figure 6-1).

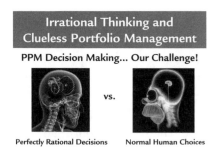

FIGURE 6-1: Irrational Thinking and Clueless Portfolio Management

A quick scan of these behavioral influences (see Figure 6-2) gives a preview of the psychological minefield. The behavioral economists argue that humans have developed these behaviors specifically to deal with complexity and uncertainty. Without these behaviors, apparently we'd be dead in the water in trying to make decisions.

- **Cumulative prospect effect:** We tend to overweight the extremes of perceived uncertainty and risk, and we tend to underweight the normal.
- **Pseudocertainty effect:** The way a scenario is portrayed can influence the decision outcome. The acceptance of a scenario is influenced by the data, its quality and the rationality of analysis, and... good-looking PowerPoint decks!
- **Framing effect:** The difference in reference points can affect decisions and actions. The $1 million difference between a $1MM project and a $2MM project will tend to influence different decisions than the same difference between a $89MM project and a $90MM project. Yet it is the same $1MM.
- **Overconfidence:** We tend to think that we're smarter than we really are. Research suggests that when we say we are 90% sure, we are more likely to be only 70%.
- **Selective memory representativeness:** We tend to weight and react to recent data much more than past/older data.

- **Loss aversion:** We tend to want to fix problem projects rather than terminating them and taking our loss.
- **Sunk cost influence:** While sunk costs are those that we will never recover, we tend to weight them in decisions even though they should be irrelevant.

FIGURE 6-2:   Microeconomic Behaviors Influencing Rational Analytics

Consider typical discussions in portfolio management meetings about the risk on one project within the portfolio. A project that is very risky can skew the discussion of the entire portfolio, regardless of the projects with normal risk levels. This is because of the behavior that some economists refer to as *cumulative prospect effect*. Indeed, there are a number of these natural "irrational" behaviors that can influence portfolio decision-making (see Figure 6-2). Portfolio managers need to recognize these behaviors if they wish to improve their organization's portfolio decision-making capability.

No doubt we should be striving to move from irrational to rational decision-making. The good news is that the negative effects of behavioral (irrational) economics on good decision-making go away as organizations build experience with the relevant decision types and with taming of the complexity and uncertainty of the data. In other words, experience and accumulated knowledge moves decisionmakers toward rational decision-making and away from behaviorally influenced decision-making. The diagram in Figure 6-3 says it all.

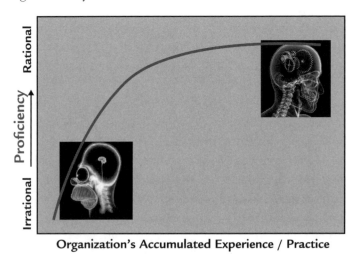

FIGURE 6-3:   Advancing from Irrational to Rational Portfolio Decision-Making

The journey from irrational to rational decision-making needs to be led by those responsible for NPD portfolio management. Sure, data quality and those software systems that help drive data quality are very important. Yet experience and knowledge are also very important. Those leading the effort need to be fluent in both the rational analytics and the irrational behavior side of portfolio decisions. But they need to get experience and knowledge transferred to the decisionmakers. The economic value of moving from irrational to rational decision-making can be quite large.

Call to Action

Please consider learning directly from a workshop on the topic and not being afraid to get your hands dirty in the muck of portfolio data. As you will see, you and your organization can move from the Homer Simpson approach to the rational thinking approach to portfolio management. But first, you should understand what you are dealing with and how to lead your organization in the transition.

NEGOTIATING SKILLS

TOOLSET: BEST PRACTICES FOR THE NEGOTIATING LIFE CYCLE

Negotiating is one of the daily tasks of the complete project manager. Apply the following best practices as you work through the negotiating life cycle.

What To Do	How To Do It
Decide to negotiate	• Find out what the issue is • Define the problem • Decide whether you need to negotiate, dominate, acquiesce, or avoid
Prepare	• Try to understand the problem, then define the goals you want to achieve • Build the necessary relationships to negotiate • Understand who is involved and their roles • Research discipline, industry, or customary standards • Define your best alternative to negotiate and improve it • Define the other party's best alternative to negotiate and worsen it

Negotiate	• Generate alternatives
	• Evaluate alternatives
	• Select the best alternative
	• Reiterate agreements
	• Capture agreements in writing
	• Create an action plan and timeline
Execute	• Congratulate the other parties
	• Follow up to assure the action plan is implemented
	• Carry out the agreed-upon solution
Follow up	• Nurture relationships
	• Check compliance with negotiated terms

TOOLSET: APPLYING NEGOTIATING RULES

The examples below illustrate ways in which the ten rules of negotiating might apply in a project management environment.

Rule	Project Management Example
1. Be patient	Dealing with a team member who is underperforming—and perhaps defensive—may be uncomfortable for a project manager, so the tendency is to get the encounter over with as quickly as possible. A better approach is to develop rapport with the person, ask for permission to provide feedback or suggestions, carefully answer any questions that come up, and take the time to reach a satisfactory agreement.
2. Be positive	A principle of persuasive influence is to deal with people you like. Having a positive attitude when interacting with project sponsors helps build confidence and credibility in their minds. This means they will engage more willingly with you in supporting the project and maintaining that support throughout the project life cycle.
3. Gather information	Clients or customers have challenges that may be addressed by the outcome of the project. Ask probing questions about what they are doing—and listen to the answers. Review the relationship history, especially if support issues have come up; determine whether or not they were adequately addressed. Find out clients' timetable or deadline, both to purchase and then to implement the solution.
4. Float trial balloons	Ask "What if we could provide key features in Phase 1 and address other wants in later phases?" These questions make no commitments but do explore reactions from the other party about possible approaches they may be willing to consider.
5. Know your status	Project managers are closest to the action on most projects and have significant status, attributable to the information they possess. Other stakeholders have status via the authority they have to allocate resources or dispense funds. There is a real opportunity to achieve better outcomes when one side is anxious to reach agreement; the other side may then nibble to gain additional concessions, perhaps by extending a resource's time on the project or reducing features in order to meet cost or time pressures.

6. Know your opening offer	You estimate a project will take between 4 to 6 months, and the customer may say that they want it in 8 months, in which case there is a cushion. But if you were aggressive and quoted first, saying the project would take 4 months (the bottom line), there would be no room to negotiate. Conversely, if the customer has no clue and thinks you can deliver the project in 2 months, open first by quoting 6 months (the edge of the envelope). You will then have room to negotiate something in between.
7. Limit your authority	Try to negotiate with the decisionmaker so that you deal with them directly and get agreement quickly. When you are the decisionmaker, have someone else negotiate on your behalf so that you cannot be pinned down by hardcore negotiating tactics. This provides opportunity to practice patience, review the proposal more thoroughly (instead of in an emotional moment), and come back with counterproposals.
8. Know your bottom line	Two vendors have similar products; one has a slight edge and costs more. You want the better product but have a strict budget limit of $10K. Negotiations with the higher-priced vendor proceed in order to get a lower price or arrange terms that fall within the budget limit. Use the limit to stand firm, negotiate with due diligence, and fall back on the other vendor if not successful. Knowing these limits allows you to determine whether to continue or walk away.
9. Be prepared	Have a risk management plan that provides advance notice of technology that may not work or tasks that could take longer than planned. Clear trigger points invoke contingency plans calling for negotiations on the pros and cons of various options, leading to quick resolution. Preparation helps you avoid being caught by surprise and having to invent options where none previously existed.
10. Never reward intimidation tactics	A PM who does not push back against unreasonable scope, schedules, or resources is training sponsors to continue such demanding behavior. Instead, set expectations by negotiating the triple constraints at project start-up and when changes occur. Make concessions when the other side makes them as well. Do not give in to intimidation tactics, or "the beatings will continue until morale improves."

TOOLSET: NEGOTIATING TESTIMONIALS

Online students in a management and leadership course provided these stories about their experiences communicating with others and negotiating for results in a project environment:

Aruna says,

> How long it takes to negotiate to set the tone depends on how willing the other party is and what other avenues one needs to take to reach the goal of communicating with them. In the case of some people, any time I try to explain anything, even before I complete my sentence, the person assumes she knows what I am about to say and interrupts by giving her opinion in a harsh or condescending way. At first, I was nice to them, and I had a feeling they took it as a sign of weakness. Now I talk to them in a very firm manner and to my surprise, it works. I should have done that from the start. Well… you learn as you go along. However, that would not be my initial choice.
>
> People come with different personalities. One has to understand and communicate with them accordingly. I learned that with difficult people one needs to set some ground rules in order to achieve your objective. I learned that by expressing my own goals openly and clarifying and confirming that the person understood what is being said, my point is being acknowledged. Even then, it would not be my first choice to set a harsh tone with certain people at work. But I felt my approach worked and I chose it after using several other communication techniques such as treating them with respect, thinking along with them by being open minded, listening to what they had to say, etc.
>
> I tried to avoid being in the same state of mind as they are by arguing. They love to argue even when there is no need to. As Zachary Wong mentions in his book (2008), "an argumentative behavior is usually a sign of insecurity, worry, and concern about their thinking." These are people who are in the same position for 15 to 20 years, and they have control issues.
>
> To deal with so-called Rational people, I actually drew a rough flow chart with a comical conclusion based on lessons I learned from previous classes. This is on one of my white boards, and it is still there to this day. When people come to talk to me, they see the picture and start laughing with approval.

HUMOR IS A GOOD VEHICLE FOR IRRATIONALITY!!!

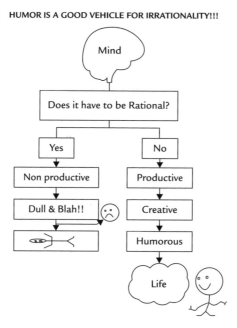

Sylvia says,

A negotiator needs to understand the value of what is being negotiated. Based on my experience, I have found that negotiating is best when you can listen with an open mind, show respect and patience, and not take anything personal. I have learned from my past experiences that negotiation is a give and take, and that you need to know the subject matter well to gauge what you can live without.

When I first started in this business, I did not understand the importance of listening, understanding, and patience, but rather concentrated on being competitive. I attribute that to my young age and lack of understanding. I found that this resulted in hurting my business relationships. My "a-ha" moment was when I collaborated with a project manager who was competitive, negative, and aggressive, and I could see how team members reacted to her. Subsequently, she had difficulty getting cooperation and meeting tasks on scheduled due dates. By witnessing her experience, and working with others who have displayed the art of negotiating, I have gained insight to the value of patience, respect, and building relationships. I believe we can compromise and still work toward a win-win result.

Wilfred says,

In my experience, being a "successful" negotiator really depends on one's definition of success. I have negotiated what I considered "successfully" at the time, only to find that what I was asked to negotiate for was not actually as beneficial as what I negotiated against.

My definition of "successful" negotiation has drastically changed over the years. In the beginning, I approached it almost like a debate team. I measured success as convincing my "opposition" to see my point of view, or the parties which I represented. This is a rather narrow-minded way of negotiating, and while it generates results, it does not foster the best environment and could sever some potentially important relationships.

Nowadays, I have a new view on successful negotiating. The most important skill that a negotiator needs in my opinion is the ability to judge the importance and long-term effects of the negotiation, not so much the topic of negotiation. Sometimes it should be seen more as coming to a mutual understanding. There are of course other times when it is still important to negotiate more aggressively for what you believe in. The art of negotiating falls in assessing the value of what you are negotiating for, and how hard you should fight for it.

Business relationships need to be a give-and-take relationship. Being too one-sided will not grow the relationship. It is natural for people to be competitive. In my case, there are many situations where I was blinded by my competitive nature and negotiated for things I did not believe in, but for the sake of negotiating. It is important to be level-headed, and extra flexible when necessary. A great mantra I repeat in my head when negotiating is "Pick your battles." You will never win them all, nor should you always want to. Learning to accept that is not accepting defeat, it is gaining wisdom and insight.

Dan replied,

Hi Wilfred,

I appreciate your advice to not be too competitive in negotiations and to pick your battles. Even if we concede on a position, it can help in the future by building a working relationship. The person or team you conceded to will remember receiving your support and would hopefully return the favor in the future. I agree that negotiation is not always about winning, but it sure can feel like it sometimes. I like how you state recognizing that your position may not always be the best, even though it is your position. To take a step back and look at the different viewpoints objectively, you can make better determinations and negotiate in that situation more effectively—because you've considered all positions.

Thanks for sharing.

TOOLSET: SPONSOR EVALUATION TOOL

Negotiations always benefit from assessment data that reveal strengths and opportunities. The purpose of this evaluation is to measure how well the sponsor supports project management in your organization. The following questions refer to a current project.

If you are not now working on a project, or if your current project has just begun and you feel you cannot answer the questions appropriately, then refer to the last project you worked on when answering these questions. If you are an upper manager, think of the project or projects with which you are most closely associated.

Respond to each statement with a score of 1 to 7 using the following scoring guidelines, and write that score in the My Score column.

1: Strongly disagree

2: Disagree

3: Somewhat disagree

4: Neutral

5: Somewhat agree

6: Agree

7: Strongly agree

A benchmark report is available from englundr@englundpmc.com that shows cumulative means and a percentile chart from people worldwide who have completed this survey. Also see www.projectsponsorship.com.

Question	My Score (1–7)	Benchmark Mean
1. The sponsor's goals for the project are clear.		
2. The sponsor believes there is a real need for the project.		
3. The sponsor understands how many people or groups will be affected by the project.		
4. The sponsor understands what resources are needed for the project to be successful.		
5. The sponsor is willing to commit the resources needed for the project to succeed.		

6. The sponsor publicly conveys the organization's strong commitment to the project and its desired outcomes.		
7. The sponsor uses appropriate rewards and pressures to gain support for the project.		
8. The sponsor ensures that procedures to track progress and problems are established.		
9. The sponsor is aware of all commitments that are required for the project to succeed.		
10. The sponsor shows consistent, sustained support for the project.		
Total		

Sponsor Factor (70-point scale)

10–29: High risk/danger

30–49: Moderate/caution

50–70: Low risk/opportunity

Success Assessment

While the purpose of the survey is to measure how well sponsors support project management in your organization, the ultimate benefit being sought is for each project to be successful and contribute value to the organization. The goal of capturing benchmarking data is to correlate component factors with project success.

Assess how well this project has succeeded or has the potential to succeed if it is currently in process. Use these criteria:

1: Project did not accomplish any of its objectives.

2: Project met only one of its objectives.

3: Project met some of its objectives.

4: Project satisfied the triple constraints of scope, schedule, and resources.

5: Project fully satisfied customer, user, or client requirements.

6: Over time, the project contributed significant value, exceeding expectations.

7: Project met or exceeded key stakeholder requirements and contributed value and benefits far in excess of its costs.

The project was a complete success (pick one):

1:   Strongly disagree
2:   Disagree
3:   Somewhat disagree
4:   Neutral
5:   Somewhat agree
6:   Agree
7:   Strongly agree

Interpreting Sponsor Factor Scores

Low risk/opportunity (50–70)

- Sponsor commitment is at the level necessary for successful change implementation.
- Extend sponsorship opportunities.

Moderate risk/caution (30–49)

- The sponsor may have an intellectual commitment to the change but fail to grasp the full meaning of what is necessary for successful implementation.
- Sponsor support for the change could deteriorate rapidly and with little warning.
- A significant amount of time and effort will need to be invested in sponsor education and maintenance.

High risk/danger (10–29)

- Strengthen sponsorship.
- Identify alternative sponsorship.
- Prepare to fail.

Success starts with a strong commitment to improve. Leaders become better prepared as sponsors of work by taking inventory of their talents, skills, and behaviors and putting appropriate action plans in place. They need to acquire skills and knowledge to transition from commander to sponsor. Knowledge management encompasses the ascent of a metaphorical stairway from data to information to knowledge and wisdom.

An objective is to unlock and open the door of sponsorship. Reaching the doors at the top of a stairway represents enlightenment—eyes are fully open about why, what, and how to invoke excellence in sponsorship. The seeker has choices: ignore the opportunities the open door represents... approach it cautiously...or pass through it eagerly. As you stand before an open door, you can spend time and energy on non-value-adding activities...or embrace sponsor and management commitments that achieve greater success.

Sponsorship is a required and critical success factor for all projects and most all work, in all industries and disciplines. Executives need training, experience, and practice to be effective sponsors. Most of all, they need followers who urge them to be better sponsors and care enough to help them move forward. Believe that every day is a good day for change.

Excellence in sponsorship needs to be every manager's mantra for achieving more within the organization.

(Adapted from Englund and Bucero 2006)

Surveys and data gathering are useful tools to establish awareness of a problem. A quick tool to assess current sponsorship is to pick one answer from the following options:

A. What sponsor?

B. Sponsor started the project but then disappeared until…

C. Sponsor was too distant to be helpful.

D. Sponsor tended to micromanage the project.

E. Sponsor was moderately helpful.

F. Sponsor made it clear what was needed and assisted in every way to make that happen.

G. Sponsor defined the project, identified constraints, funded the project with adequate resources, made timely decisions, resolved conflicts, and supported the team throughout the project.

Obviously, the preferred answer is response G, or something close to it. In most groups where we have conducted this quiz, we get a normal distribution with the peak in the middle between slightly negative and slightly positive responses. Most often there will be one or two people whose sponsors reach the ideal definition in G. Those people describe environments where very enlightened managers successfully transitioned from commander to sponsor.

Moving from A to G takes awareness and explicit commitments to make changes and continuously improve the sponsorship role. Use a quiz like this to measure progress. Rely on positive examples and dialogue, coupled with patience and persistence, to stay the course.

TOOLSET: NEGOTIATING TECHNIQUES

Here are some specific suggestions for negotiating in a project environment:

- Assure the project is properly chartered and sponsored.
- Establish clear company priorities, with buy-in and support from the sponsor and leadership team.
- Locate project results within company priorities.
- Tie project goals and results to supporting business goals.
- Clearly define and vividly illustrate the tasks required to reach project goals.
- Clearly define and vividly illustrate project resource requirements.
- Build trust and credibility through accurate project planning and schedules and open and honest communication.
- Provide risk assessments for missing resources.
- Know the cost of delay.
- Quantify the cost of *not* having the resources required.

Here are ten additional negotiating techniques:

1. Make the pie bigger.
2. Use humor.
3. Show your strength.
4. Ask a question.
5. Review your preparation (privately).
6. Breathe deeply.
7. Name hard-line tactics.
8. Take a break.
9. Use silence (after explaining your proposal).
10. Reframe an issue.

TOOLSET: "COURAGEOUS" DECISIONS IN NEGOTIATION

Noted for his stimulating and innovative presentations at PMI Global Congresses, Crispin ("Kik") Piney, PgMP, has an interesting approach to negotiating challenging demands that come from sponsors:

> One of the most sensitive areas of negotiation for project managers is when the sponsor is asking for a feature or change that the project manager feels would put main project objectives at risk. The challenge for the project manager is to be able to refuse the request, or get it changed without damaging on-going relationships with the sponsor: don't say no, say "yes, but ...."

But what?

For the "but" to be meaningful to the sponsor, it needs to have two major characteristics:

- It relates directly to the interests of the sponsor: saying "Yes, but it will make my job more difficult" is not a useful comment and could well generate an answer of the type: "I expect you to rise to the challenge—that's part of your job description."
- It is backed up by well-documented, objective data: soft skills work best when based on hard data.

So, how could you do this?

Start from a complete and valid project model. This includes, for example, a sufficiently detailed schedule, including information from a risk analysis of the corresponding risks. The benefit of such a model is that the project manager can apply it to develop the following data for use in future negotiations:

- Curves providing the relationship between target dates and confidence levels. In the same way as for modern weather forecasts, this leads to statements such as "Aiming for a handover date of 1 May 2012 exposes the project to a 20 percent risk of schedule overrun."
- Scenario analysis can be carried out rapidly and reliably, for example, "Reducing the resources available in a given category would change our chances of finishing on time from 80 percent to 40 percent."

Once you have these analysis capabilities—using, for example, Monte Carlo analysis—you are fully armed with the requisite data. Now you can use it to negotiate as an "advisor" for your sponsor.

As mentioned above, do not say no. Take a lesson in the use of language from the British television show *Yes Minister*, written by Antony Jay and Jonathan Lynn. The advisor to the minister begins:

Sir Humphrey: If you want to be really sure that the minister doesn't accept it, you must say the decision is "courageous."

Bernard: And that's worse than "controversial"?

Sir Humphrey: Oh, yes! "Controversial" only means "this will lose you votes." "Courageous" means "this will lose you the election!"

Similarly, in the project area, the project manager needs to ensure that the sponsor knows if a request is "controversial" or, at the limit, "courageous." Use a simple statement—based on solid analysis—of the type, "I do take my hat off to your courageous decision to accept personal responsibility for having reduced the chances of project success, based on your public commitments, from 80 percent to 10 percent... and being willing to defend this decision in the (very likely) event of project failure."

This is win-win for the project manager. If the decision is maintained, the sponsor is a full partner in sharing—and managing—the risk; if the request is modified, the decision to do so comes from the sponsor, so the sponsor is a full partner in the decision rather than an unwilling victim. This approach should lead to better decisions and to an enhanced relationship with the sponsor.

TOOLSET: STAKEHOLDER MANAGEMENT SKILLS

Personal examples often map onto project management practices. When a flood drove her from her house in the UK, Sheilina Somani, FAPM, PMP, owner of Positively Project Management, found her finely honed stakeholder management skills came in handy (2011):

> I've been reviewing lessons learned as I plan my family's move back. I was fully insured, and my important papers were protected and easily accessible. Then reality began to sink in. I was faced with numerous stakeholders and decisionmakers who all had the ability to speed or slow the project to return back home. And I had no official project management title or role to fall back on.
>
> The stakeholders included: insurance representatives, loss adjusters, drying specialists, cleaners, builders, electricians, removal companies, renovators, family, friends, neighbors, police, water and supply companies, and the local council. Then there were ancillary people, such as credit card representatives, bank employees, and business and school contacts.
>
> All these stakeholders to manage—and I had to continue running two large projects at work and be a parent.

Much at Stake

The project to return home is going to be long, but I am determined. While each stakeholder has an interest in the project, only I have a passion in ensuring its timely conclusion. I've been able to apply several project management skills toward that end:

- **Communication:** Treat people courteously. Ask many questions and seek continuous clarification, provide feedback—and then ask more questions.
- **Organization:** Monitor who relates to whom and how each group interacts.
- **Documentation:** Track correspondence and dates, and ask all critical questions in writing (leaving an audit trail as a result).
- **Honesty and openness:** Declare a lack of knowledge up front and ask for patience as people explain the necessary details.
- **Sense of scope:** No one precious to me was hurt, which means the project details are relatively straightforward.

As an experienced project manager, I have the skills to recognize the differing goals and drivers of the stakeholder groups, and the need to communicate in terms of win-win approaches for everyone. The challenge is to keep everyone focused on our need to return home, and do so without becoming an irritant. Because I try to be respectful of the various skills of the people who surround me, they're more willing to share their expertise. This has been invaluable to me as a novice in a crisis.

By April, we'll be halfway through what is likely to be a 10-month project. It has taken a significant mental, physical emotional and, of course, financial toll on us, but my experience as a project manager has helped reduce the stress.

In my personal and professional circles, I employ project management skills regularly with humor and confidence. But never have they been more useful than over the past few months—giving me at least some semblance of sanity when I'm surrounded by so much uncertainty.

POLITICAL SKILLS

TOOLSET: COMPETENCE

A first key to political success is being perceived as competent. What does it take to be a competent project manager? Dr. J. Davidson Frame provides this list in his book, *Building Project Management Competence* (1999):

- Be a results-oriented, can-do individual
- Have a head for details
- Possess a strong commitment to the project
- Be aware of the organization's goals
- Be politically savvy
- Be cost conscious
- Understand business basics
- Be capable of understanding the needs of staff, customers, and management
- Be capable of coping with ambiguity, setbacks, and disappointments
- Possess good negotiation skills
- Possess the appropriate technical skills to do his or her job.

From the top down, this list highlights the major contribution made by project managers and project management and what complete project managers never forget: we get the job done! This profession is all about getting results.

TOOLSET: THE DISCOVERY PROCESS USING APPRECIATIVE INQUIRY

Improving political skills may involve a change in thinking about how to discover and appreciate what is really going on in the organization. Organizations and people do not need to be "fixed." Avoid a "deficit discourse" that dwells on what is wrong or needs to be developed. Instead, discover strengths. Establish shared values and put them into practice.

In order to prevent people believing they need to resort to political means in order to attract attention, exert power, or get their way, take the time to emphasize the importance of each person's contribution and how that person contributes to the organization. Do this early in each project.

Use the power of feedback: make it a high priority to respond to every inquiry; share what thinking processes are going on; develop and use consistent criteria for decision-making; communicate all news, whether good or bad; provide reflective answers to questions; tame anxiety responses and provide space for others to come through; and generally become known for quality responses.

Appreciate the ebb and flow of team dynamics—using discretion about when to push and when to let a natural energy drive the process.

These steps demonstrate that the leader is paying attention to the people responsible for success.

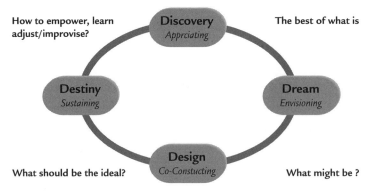

FIGURE 8-1:   The Four Ds of Appreciative Inquiry

Adapted from Cooperrider and Whitney, *Appreciative Inquiry* (2000)

Appreciative inquiry (Cooperrider and Whitney 2000) is a discipline that guides a focus on people and organizational strengths. Figure 8-1 shows how to approach work and changes within any organization using appreciative inquiry.

For instance, one client wanted to develop a more cohesive project team. I (Englund) conducted exploratory interviews across the organization. The first step, the *discovery* approach, involved interviewing each member using the following questions:

- What attracted you to this team? (initial excitements, impressions)
- What do you value most—about yourself, your job, the organization?
- What are the core values of this organization, the key things without which this organization would not exist?
- Recall a time when you felt most alive, involved, joyful, in peak form, or excited:
    - What made it an exciting experience?
    - Who were the most significant others involved?
    - Why were they significant?
    - Tell a story about that time (what were you doing, what others did, how you felt)
- What was the most exciting, surprising, or humorous thing that has occurred with this team?
- What is the single most important thing the team has contributed to your life?
- What is the essence or life-giving force of this team?
- What could (or should) be the most important outcome from your experiences with this team?

Some responses about what people appreciate in the organization illustrate the strengths and common values people shared:

- Appreciate that people are not pigeon-holed, OK to go out of scope of job, do the right thing, not cutting corners
- Bug people to move out of status quo, see gems, winners
- Financial responsibility, sense of being in wealth, pushing human capacity
- Leading international team responsible for standardizing processes across multiple countries—wonderful team, motivated, worked things out, political but straightforward, wonderful management support, room to make decisions, did what others said couldn't be done
- Understood organization and political environment, well respected by peers, could get job done, believed in mission, committed, willing to fight for vision
- Huge stake in delivering something, all given little piece, expectations set to deliver, cohesive group, working in real time, complex
- Without them [our leaders], we wouldn't be around, all on same vision, they were living the vision with us and embracing it
- They took idea, delivered on promise or went further; others are doing it, expansion; trust that others do well, respect, meaningful way to operate

- I was put into situation I did not want to be in, said to boss "take me out of it"; boss talked me into it; case became very clear w/ data; turnaround occurred after the project was over, frightening, got so involved, came to realize I am the best person, drew upon strengths; presentation weary, practiced with team leader, got coaching

- Accidental project manager, shared passion and vision carried us through— became "my vision," common vision, trust

- Group brought together with varied experience, given huge responsibility that would change how entire company operated, opportunity to learn about people, challenging issues, HR skills acquired, rose to the occasion, amazing

- All people were there, displayed visions, kept reinforcing with actual items, possible because highest level of management support [said] "yes, this will work," true management buy-in, getting smoother, projecting issues and solutions, empowered (not passive), work getting done; enthusiasm, measures of success—quantitative and qualitative, believed what doing, hired very good people—came because heard of us, type of organization being built, vision and values, zero turnover

A second step is to *dream* of a more desired future state. This step involves finding ways to reinforce existing strengths and positive work experiences. This is especially relevant to our example, the first step of which revealed that people thoroughly enjoyed intense activities directed toward an important goal. This discovery was in sharp contrast to a common perception that people want to avoid stressful situations. We learned that these situations are when people feel truly engaged.

The next step was to focus in facilitated sessions on crafting powerful purpose, vision, values, and mission statements that become living, breathing statements to guide all members of the community on a common path. The group was ready for this work because they identified that they needed a common vision and wanted a better view of the bigger picture. In these sessions, we adopted "ground rules":

- Each person accountable for success of:
  - This session
  - Ongoing team development
- Able and willing to:
  - Influence
  - Be influenced
- Suspend sense of certainty; be open to new ways of thinking

The third step, *design*, is to assign or write and review role and responsibility guidelines. We scheduled sessions across the organization to share statements and results of interviews that reflected what was working well and what could be when those behaviors were reinforced.

The agenda for this session looked like this:

- Summarize interviews
- Share stories
- Review models
- Decide what is needed
- Use tools
- Draft operating statements
- Agree on action plan.

Encourage inquiry and dialogue so people believe and commit to this approach.

The fourth step, *destiny*, is to act on the new design, reinforce it through training and practice sessions, and reap the benefits of people operating within their strengths. After a while, it becomes important once again to reassess what is going on and determine if new capabilities have been discovered. The outcome of this step was a simple but elegant statement of operating principles, as depicted in Figure 8-2.

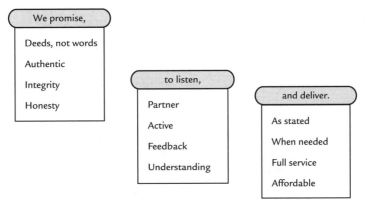

FIGURE 8-2: Organizational Operating Principles

The appreciative inquiry tool is so powerful that it can even dwarf or minimize the need to point out what people do wrong. By reinforcing strengths, weaknesses fall by the wayside. These steps also cut through the political maneuverings that so often happen by making them unnecessary.

TOOLSET: MAPPING STAKEHOLDERS' BEHAVIOR

Stakeholder analysis is integral to developing a political plan. One way to do this is to apply traits or characteristics of animals to people within the organization. This has proven to be a fun and less risky approach to sensitive topics. People quickly come to understand the challenges of dealing with these "animals."

You can begin by assessing each individual on the degree of mutual trust and on his or her agreement with the project or program's purpose, vision, and mission. That puts each person in one of four quadrants (see Figure 8-3):

- High agreement, high trust: Allies
- High agreement, low trust: Comrades
- Low agreement, high trust: Opponents
- Low agreement, low trust: Adversaries

Then determine what "animal" they are. Most "animals" can fall into any quadrant.

- **Tiger:** Solitary, powerful, strong and skillful.
- **Lion:** Social, outgoing, approachable, "roars" to make claims.
- **Bear:** Solitary, intelligent, avoids people.
- **Venomous snake:** Cold-blooded, ruthless when provoked.
- **Female black widow spider:** Shy and solitary but venomous; eats weaker colleagues for breakfast.
- **Arctic fox:** Easy to recognize but hard to catch; manipulates with a smile.
- **Sheep:** Herds animals; follows leaders willingly and produces what is required.

FIGURE 8-3: Stakeholder Trust and Agreement Matrix

Ultimately, the goal is to move everyone up and to the right—into the allies quadrant—on the grid. Start by reinforcing positions of strength and then work on areas of concern. Use your knowledge about each "animal's" traits and behavior patterns to address each stakeholder's needs—and to protect yourself when necessary. Realize that different "animals" speak different languages, so the complete project manager needs to become multilingual, meaning that you have to adapt your language to whatever is most comfortable and customary for the person with whom you are speaking.

TOOLSET: POWER STRUCTURE

Begin improving your political skills by understanding the power structure and decision-making processes in your organization. Do this by analyzing how things get done:

- Sources of power
  - **Position power** is the title conferred by the organization on an individual that carries defined responsibility and authority.
  - **Information power** is the access that a person has to who, what, when, or where things are happening.
  - **Contact power** comes from a wide base of people a person knows and can summon for specific interactions.
  - **Network power** is a wide web of contacts to access information or authority.
  - **Situation power** comes in the moment; an individual has certain skills that are needed in particular circumstances.
  - **Personal power** pertains to the emotional, charismatic, personality, or other features that are attractive and effective within an individual.
- Credibility
  - **Networking credibility** is the ability to access high-quality working relationships, to identify where better relationships are required, and to develop a wider support network when needed.
  - **Relationship credibility** is the ability to connect with others and get reciprocal responses due to sincerity and personal effectiveness.
  - **Knowledge credibility** means being on top of the latest accurate and reliable information and sharing it with integrity.
- Where, who, and how decisions are made
- Critical stakeholders:
  - Sponsor, dependent, participant
  - "Who could stop this effort?"
- Develop a different approach to each stakeholder based upon diagnoses from previous steps:
  - Leverage your strengths
  - Build support
- Build a guiding coalition
  - Develop dedicated grassroots effort
  - Enlist support of powerful sponsors
- Focus efforts on areas that are:
  - Central or visible to other corporate members
  - Important for organizational goals

- – Tied into resource allocation
- Demonstrate legitimacy and expertise by:
  - – Developing proficiency
  - – Employing best practices
  - – Communicating successes
- Use your cultural context to decide if you should develop the political plan by yourself or with a team and if it can be shared in public or kept private. If your organization is closed and highly political, proceed with caution. An open, enlightened organization allows for inputs, findings, and recommendations to be accessible by and useful for all stakeholders.
- Document the findings in a plan (see templates in this book and on the web at www.englundpmc.com under Offerings) that includes:
  - – Assessment of environment
  - – Description of political jungle
  - – Stakeholder roles
  - – Potential issues
  - – Approach to stakeholders and issues
  - – Strategic response, such as positioning and steps to take
  - – Action plans
- Act on the plan.

TOOLSET: SAMPLE POLITICAL PLAN

My [SAMPLE] Political Plan

- Assessment of environment
  We are a "loose-tight" organization with a moderately weak project culture. Power is relatively diffused, and no one person dominates team meetings. People with initiative can step up and succeed, but few of these efforts are coordinated across the organization. Ineffective and inefficient processes are a big problem.

- Description of political jungle
  The tigers stay out of our way. The lions' roars are not heard very far, and the bears seem to run the show, doing their own thing. Venomous attacks can come from anywhere, especially when traversing in new territories.

- Stakeholder roles
  Sponsors are assigned but do not actively support projects unless asked. Team members lack full commitment to the project because of other distractions. Senior management is just beginning to understand the value of project and program management to the vitality of the organization.

- Potential issues
  Working on too many projects threatens successful completion. Requirements change when managers cater to special interests. Vague understanding of roles and responsibilities creates confusion and leads to missed milestones. Few commitments exist to follow through on project plans.

- Approach to stakeholders and issues
  Need to get tigers involved in supporting program management and a project portfolio process. Need to harness the lions to roar in concert by focusing on a limited set of strategic goals and corresponding projects. The bears will continue to perform as long as we do not disturb them too much with complex processes or detailed checklists.

- Strategic response, such as positioning and steps
  A small project office reporting to the general manager can facilitate the introduction of simple portfolio and project management processes. Get the attention of the lions by pointing out the consequences in the market if we fail to systematically coordinate our efforts. Neutralize negative (venomous) behaviors with an open approach to all issues and the free flow of information.

- Action plans
  Interview all stakeholders. Prepare proposal. Line up upper management support. Define the project sponsor role and conduct training for new sponsors. Develop an environment where excellence in project sponsorship contributes to competitive advantage. Select strategic efforts leading first to small wins before rolling out more broadly. Get explicit commitments from all stakeholders. Remember to be authentic and act with integrity on every interaction.

©Randall L. Englund, www.englundpmc.com

TOOLSET: SHIFTING THE BURDEN

In systems thinking terms, the predicament caused by vicious loops can be understood as a classic example of a "shifting the burden" archetype (Senge 2006, 103–110). Such an archetype is a pattern that helps explain recurring behaviors in human interactions. Shifting the burden is when applying a short-term fix actually undermines a leader's ability to take action at a more fundamental level.

The causal loop, starting in the middle of Figure 8-4, depicts how many project leaders proceed when under pressure to get results. The quick fix (in balancing loop B1) is to resort to a command-and-control approach, which on a surface level appears to lessen the pressure. However, this approach drives individuals to commit "integrity crimes"—they believe that what they say is more important than what they do. This has an opposite effect on the people they want to influence or persuade (in reinforcing loop R3). These people do not do their best work, so more pressure is felt to get results.

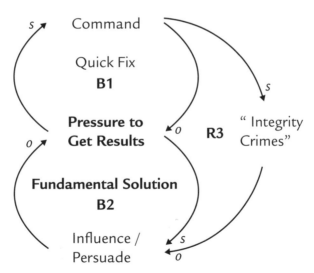

FIGURE 8-4: A "Shifting the Burden" Causal Loop

The fundamental solution to the pressure to get results is to develop skills of persuasion as practiced by a change agent (in balancing loop B2). Help people come to believe in the vision and mission and to figure out why it is in their best interest to put their best work into the project. People usually respond positively to this approach and accomplish the work with less pressure. Tap the innate talents residing in people and create a natural living-system environment where people and information move freely. This virtuous loop represents a political plan at its finest.

Mapping behaviors shows how what we do comes back to help or hurt us. It also shows the ripple effect of multiple actions, in other words, how interdependent we are. Feedback is also a powerful tool to guide behavior. These tools reinforce the need to be careful in what we do when interacting with others and also the power of changing behaviors simply by giving feedback to others about the consequences of their actions. This leads to self-correcting behaviors.

Consider these steps:

- Identify basic leadership traits and their consequences; know yourself.
- Assess and compare leadership approaches in complex situations; practice developing judgment by simulating what you would do and comparing that to what respected leaders actually did.
- Break a vicious loop somewhere, then apply a correction by invoking fundamental solutions, as depicted in a "shifting the burden" structure, to create a positive culture.
- Appreciate the value of authentic leadership.
- Commit to act with integrity.

Know also that leadership, and subsequent followership, depends upon the emotional bonding and alignment that occurs among people, teams, and the organization. This becomes a primary role for leading in a political environment—developing skills of emotional intelligence and practicing "primal leadership" (Goleman et al. 2002).

CONFLICT MANAGEMENT SKILLS

TOOLSET: A TECHNIQUE FOR RESOLVING CONFLICT

A technique developed by Jay Rothman (1997) is a useful way to approach and resolve conflicts at each of three levels: resource, objective, or identity (R, O, or I). The techniques apply in the world of project, programs, and portfolios, though they can be extended so far as to apply to international disputes.

The letters that make up the word ARIA each stand for a stage in the conflict resolution process: antagonism, resonance, invention, and action. (ARIA is also a musical metaphor—as in a musical aria—which alludes to the creativity needed to resolve conflict.)

The iceberg analogy (see Figure 9-1) and the ROI assessment guide which steps to use in resolving a conflict and the order in which you apply them. Go from the bottom up in the Conflict Resolution Checklist (see Figure 9-2), starting only as deep as the level of conflict. That is, a resource conflict only needs invention and then action; in an objective conflict you first need to establish resonance before proceeding to invention and action.

Because identity-based conflicts are complex and often threatening, it is important to begin the resolution process with the antagonism step. People need to express frustrations and get their emotions acknowledged before they will tolerate any rational discussion. If this step is skipped, the opportunity for disputants to address their differences and begin to understand the other side is lost. The likelihood of disputants simply "glossing over" the problem increases if the antagonism step is overlooked, resulting in an increased probability that the conflict will recur.

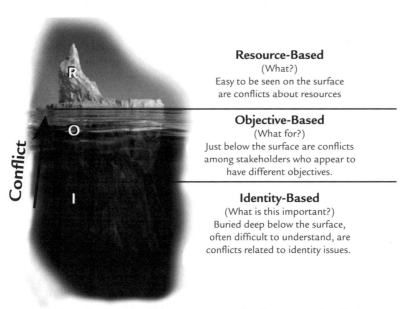

Water is like the environment in which we operate;occasionally an iceberg (conflict) appears
which can be shallow and visible or deep and extending well below the visible surface area

FIGURE 9-1:   An Iceberg Analogy for Assessing Conflicts

Conflict Resolution Checklist using ARIA	
Action	
Ask, "what, why, who, how, and when."	
Follow through!	
Invention	
Brainstorm for cooperative solutions.	
Encourage participation from all disputants.	
Resonance	
Ask, "why do disputants want what they want, and why do they care so much"	
Ask, "what is most important to each side involved in this conflict?"	
Determine where disputants share responsibility for this conflict.	
Determine which needs and values are threatened by this conflict.	
Antagonism	
Create a "safe" environment.	
Vent frustrations.	
Discuss how conflicts were handled poorly in the past.	
Listen to the other side.	

Resource
based

Objective
based

Identity
based

FIGURE 9-2:   Conflict Resolution Checklist

In workshops, I (Englund) inevitably find people who are experiencing each of
the three levels of conflict. They can then apply the checklist to real-life examples,
which reveals the usefulness of this approach. People discover that a systematic
approach to conflict resolution is not only possible but also very effective.

TOOLSET: TECHNIQUES TO MANAGE LOWER-LEVEL BEHAVIORS

A team's *set point* represents the collective mindset and spirit of the team. A low set point means that the team practices poor team behaviors (e.g., resistance, impatience, fearfulness, defensiveness) more often than collaborative behaviors (e.g., listening, giving to others, transparency).

What can you do if your team is mired in lower-level behaviors?

1. **Help others rise to a higher level.** The key is to give people an "upward lift": motivate people to listen, broaden their thinking, and get them to accept other possibilities and options.
   - Use a bridging process to acknowledge what other people say and do—look beyond yourself, acknowledge others, show respect, be transparent, and connect thoughts before making comments.
   - Help others get transparent—ask questions, acknowledge positive behaviors.
   - Understand personality types to improve interactions.
   - Put it in "neutral" before "drive"—shift dialogue from telling to mutual listening.
   - Pace body language, speech pattern, and tone to the other person's.
   - Treat people as if they were in their upper level.

2. **Break a negative cycle.** When stuck in a lower level, like a wheel that keeps going around, break out of it:
   - Change the mood.
   - Switch content, process, and/or behavior to restart a discussion.
   - Switch polarity—take the opposite view.

3. **Avoid dropping into the lower level.**
   - If dug in deep, know when to come up for air.
   - If someone's hot button is hit, deflect or exit right away.
   - Spin forward—say something positive that is forward looking.
   - Use intuition; speak up if something does not feel right.
   - You get what you give.
   - Know when to give up or when you are in a situation you cannot win.

Figure 9-3 summarizes these techniques.

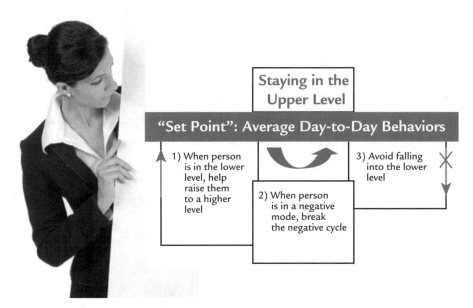

FIGURE 9-3:   Techniques to Manage Lower Set Points

Adapted from Wong, *Human Factors in Project Management* (2007)
Reprinted with permission of John Wiley & Sons, Inc.

TOOLSET: CONDUCT A LEARNING CONVERSATION

In situations that matter the most, you often perform at your worst. You choose one of the behaviors in Figure 9-4—in the extreme, either lashing out to attack the other person or avoiding him or her and staying silent. Neither is productive in most work situations.

The basic question you need to ask is, "What is at stake here?" A much more positive approach is to conduct a learning conversation, which means to engage in dialogue with a free flow of meaning. Figure 9-5 depicts the flow from challenges to options:

Here are suggested steps for achieving dialogue in a learning conversation:

- Begin from the third story—not your story or the other person's story, but how an impartial observer would describe the situation; this also could be an alternate story creating an ideal situation.

- Explain your purpose and extend an invitation. It is always wise to ask people if it is okay to give them feedback or share constructive criticism.

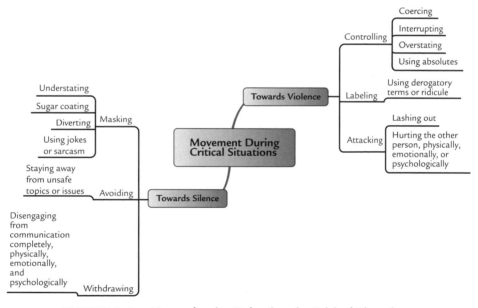

FIGURE 9-4: Unproductive Behaviors in Critical Situations

FIGURE 9-5: Conduct a Learning Conversation

- Explore their story to demonstrate empathic understanding.
- Share your own story, bringing personal learnings into the dialogue.
- Take the lead in problem-solving.

TOOLSET: REFRAMING

Reframing is seeing conflict or decisions through different lenses that each have a different frame around them. In a project management context, at its most basic, reframing means viewing project management as people management to achieve strategic goals—not just assembling tasks and timing charts.

In terms of conflict management, reframing means adding more alternatives, options, and considerations for review. A wise leader introduces reframing very early in a conflict in order to get people out of ruts and into thinking differently. This process opens doors to better compromises or creative solutions.

TABLE 9-1: Reframing Possibilities

Frame	Metaphor	Central Concept	Image of Leadership	Basic Challenge
Structural / rational	Mechanical System	Rules, roles, goals, policies, science and technology	Intelligence	Align the organization to task, technology, and environment
Human resource	Family	Needs, skills, relationships, and feelings	Empowerment	Align organizational and human needs
Political	Jungle	Power, conflict, competition, organizational politics	Advocacy	Develop an agenda and power base
Symbolic	Theater	Culture, meaning, metaphor, ritual, ceremony, stories, heroes	Inspiration	Create faith, beauty, meaning

Adapted from Bolman and Deal, *Reframing Organizations* (1997)
Reprinted with permission of John Wiley & Sons, Inc.

According to professors Lee Bolman and Terrence Deal (1997), the same situation can be viewed in at least four different ways. As depicted in Table 9-1, possible frames include structural or rational, human resource, political, and symbolic. Each frame has its own image of reality. The "secret sauce" applied by successful complete project managers is to apply multiple frames to the same—and every—situation. This technique helps you connect with reticent people who each have a different view or way of seeing the world.

As you apply all four frames in the table, you develop greater appreciation and deeper understanding of people and organizational situations. Galileo discovered this when he devised the first telescope—each lens that he added contributed to a more accurate image of the heavens. Successful managers reframe until they understand the situation at hand.

Let us apply reframing to a decision that may face managers in an organization: Should a team be colocated? Project goals may dictate that most active project team members need to be in the same physical location, where they have a team meeting room and places to post project documents and are able to develop a sense of community. Circumstances, however, might require that people operate virtually, around the globe.

- Structurally, it makes sense to have people colocate for highest performance, but financially, it may be less expensive to keep team members where they currently reside.

- The human resource frame acknowledges the necessity for face-to-face encounters to build rapport and resolve contentious issues quickly.

- Politically there may be power-based "empires" that want to protect home turfs, or local regulations requiring people to work in home locations.

- The symbolic gesture of colocating people on a high-priority project conveys a clear message that people are expected to focus on the project, work (and play) together, and complete heroic challenges.

Each frame has its pros and cons. The deciding factor may be current priorities as applied to various frames.

Multiframe thinking requires movement beyond narrow and mechanical thinking. Complete project managers who master the ability to reframe get a liberating sense of choice and power, develop unique alternatives and novel ideas about what organizations need, are better attuned to people and events, are less startled by organizational perversities, see new possibilities, determine wider ranges of outcomes dealing with uncertainty, and anticipate turbulent twists and turns of organizational life. They are like artists who reframe the world so others can see new possibilities.

SALES SKILLS

 TOOLSET: SELLING SKILLS FOR COMPLETE PROJECT MANAGERS

Figure 10-1 presents a mindmap of a complete set of skills and steps to apply when engaged in a selling process.

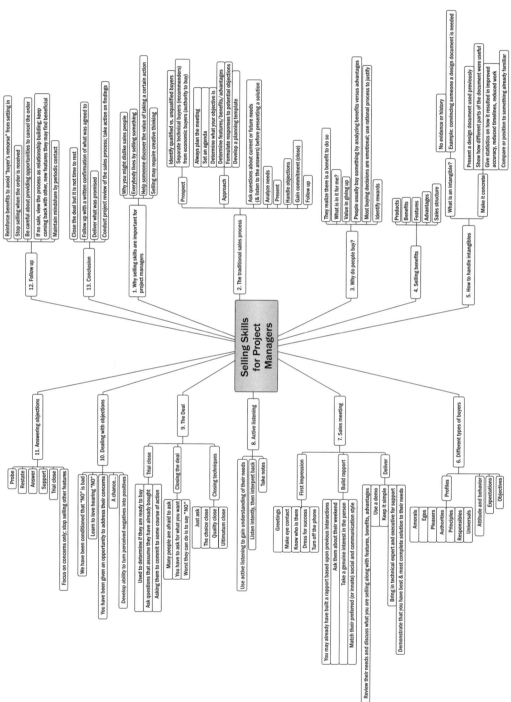

FIGURE 10-1: Mindmap of Sales Skills and Steps

TOOLSET: SALES PROPOSAL KIT

Good proposals to clients require preparation. Successful sales proposals are well planned, well written, cohesive, and competitive.

Some best practices when preparing large proposals include:

- Develop a proposal strategy that ensures a high probability of winning the contract through the proposal.
- Develop a detailed set of customer requirements and questions to be answered in the proposal.
- Develop an outline of the proposal similar to the table of contents for a textbook. Make sure you use any customer-prescribed format when developing the outline.
- Develop a writing task list for all components of the proposal.
- Assign smaller tasks with shorter time frames to writers.
- Conduct frequent reviews of the writer's work and ensure the customer's requirements and questions are being answered.
- Using the detailed outline, prepare the framework and complete the general requirements of a proposal.
- Start integrating writers' contributions early and ensure the contributions are responsive to customer requirements.
- Conduct frequent team reviews to show progress and to identify written work that needs revision or additional work to clarify the proposal.
- Assemble all written work and conduct a comprehensive review with senior management to obtain approval for release.

Here are suggested steps to put into a schedule of proposal development activities:

What To Do	How To Do It
Gather background data	Meet the salespeople or the person who will be involved in the sale and ask questions of him or her. If that is not possible, make an appointment with the customer and get as much information as possible.
Develop proposal strategy	Develop a proposal strategy that ensures a high probability of winning the contract through the proposal.

Develop proposal plan with list of tasks to be done	Break down the list of the tasks that need to be done and create a work breakdown structure, then a schedule diagram, and build up a proposal plan. The entire proposal team should work on the plan together.
Meet with all proposal team members to explain the subject and requirements	Clarify the subject of the proposal and the requirements to be addressed in the proposal. Get answers to any questions that come up.
Assign tasks to team members	Ensure that each task has an owner.
Write framework of proposal	Document and share the proposal framework with all team members.
Review writings and integrate	Review all individual writings and integrate them into the proposal text. Ensure a consistent voice.
Review complete proposal	Review all content of the proposal, taking into account team members' different points of view.
Edit proposal and prepare in final form	Edit the proposal, correct mistakes, and format the proposal.
Obtain approval and feedback from senior management	Get upper management buy-in and receive feedback from them.
Produce and prepare final copies	Print out and format final copies of the proposal.
Deliver and present to the customer	Deliver the proposal to the customer through a verbal presentation, explaining all the content and details. Plan to deliver early, allowing time for possible delays.

Proposal Content

Proposals usually address three areas for the customer:

- What are you, the performing organization, going to do?
- How are you going to manage it?
- How much will it cost?

The main components to be included are listed below. (Depending on the magnitude of the project, these components may be integrated into one document or appear in three separate documents.)

What To Do	How To Do It
Executive summary	Highlight key aspects of the proposal, similar to a project objectives statement, that says what you are doing, why, how, and how much it will cost.
Technical	Description of the work to be accomplished and the procedures used to do the work.
Management	What is the proposed method to manage this project work and the necessary information required to establish credibility?
Pricing	Proposed bid price and proposed terms and conditions.

TOOLSET: SALES PRESENTATION SKILLS

Every sales presentation must be customized to the client. These suggestions will help you do so.

What To Do	How To Do It
Be informed	Before preparing any presentation, whether it is for one person or thousands, know your purpose (inform, persuade, entertain, sell), know your audience well (demographics, attitudes, hot buttons, background), and know your logistics.
Pay attention to timing	Plan, prepare, and practice for 75% of the allotted time. If you end early, no one complains. Ending late means poor planning. If you expect some involvement from the audience, plan on talking 40% of the time and allowing 25% of the time for interaction.
Base the presentation on audience interest	All presentation material is not created equal. When preparing your talk, consider the must know, should know, and could know. Limit the material based on time or audience interest.
Use your passion	Infusing presentations with enthusiasm creates more impact and action than pure data. Include stories, analogies, metaphors, and previous experiences to reinforce key points.
Prepare user-friendly notes	Use bulleted points instead of sentences. Make the type easy to read (minimum 18 point type, boldface); use only the top two-thirds of the page so that you do not have to look down to read them.
Rehearse the presentation	Practice out loud, saying it differently each time you say it.
Be excited	No coach tells the team to be calm. Convert adrenaline into enthusiasm. Control physical symptoms by breathing from the diaphragm, using positive visualization and self-talk—and being prepared and practiced.

Deliver your presentation with enthusiasm	Deliver your talk with passion; it is amazing how much positivity enthusiasm provokes. If your voice is expressive and your gestures animated, you appear passionate and confident.
Prepare thoroughly for the question-and-answer part of the presentation	The question-and-answer part of the presentation may be more important than the actual presentation. Think ahead to all possible questions that might be asked, particularly the ones that might throw you. Paraphrase questions before answering them, and take into account the motivation of the questioner. When answering questions, look at all audience members; they may have had the same question. Avoid complimenting some questions and not others. Treat all questions and questioners with respect.
Focus on the audience, not yourself	Remember that speaking is an audience-centered sport. Avoid speaking out of ego or appearing cocky or unprepared. As long as you stay focused on the audience in preparation, delivery, and during the questions and answers, you can be successful as a presenter.

CHANGE MANAGEMENT SKILLS

Why do people resist change? Change is hard for everyone. Change is one of the greatest attitude obstacles complete project managers will face. We cannot move forward and stay the same at the same time. People resist change for several reasons:

- **Personal loss:** Whenever a change is imminent, the first question that pops into people's minds is how the change will affect them. The first critical success factor in managing resistance to change is communication. One of a project manager's key obligations is to talk to stakeholders about how a change will affect them, but this discussion often does not happen.

- **Fear of the unknown:** I (Bucero) helped a savings bank organization in Spain to increase its PM maturity level, consulting and training people on project management. Hanging on one of the walls was a poster saying, "If everything is okay, please do not change it." I explained to them that my approach as a project manager was, "If everything is okay, please worry about it, because it may be improved." Project managers need to communicate both knowns and unknowns throughout project life cycles.

- **They were not part of the decision-making or implementation design process.**

- **Bad timing.** Run through the following checklist before implementing a big change:
    - Will this change benefit the team?
    - Is the change compatible with the purpose of the project?
    - Is this change specific and clear?
    - Are the top 20 percent (the influencers) in favor of this change?
    - Is it possible to test this change before making a total commitment to it?
    - Are physical, financial, and human resources available to make this change?

- Is this change reversible?
- Is this change the next obvious step?
- Does this change have both short- and long-term benefits?

If you answer too many questions "no," then the timing may not be right to make the change.

- **Because it feels awkward.** Accepting change as a part of working on projects means exposure to a variety of new and possibly uncomfortable situations. A complete project manager is willing to experiment, assess personal and others' reactions and behaviors, and seek a path toward progress.

- **Tradition.** Many professionals have managed projects for many years without applying a formal methodology. Project results were not bad, but were not great either. As organizations grow in terms of people and project complexity, the need arises to implement a formal PM methodology.

How can your attitude be the difference maker concerning change? Think about a change you are currently resisting. It can be a change you feel prompted to make or are currently being asked to make by others. Keep in mind that for positive change to occur, you need to make a commitment to pay the price for change. Change needs to happen within you before it can happen around you. It is never too late to change. Attila is more competitive while Quaker is more collaborative.

TOOLSET: CHANGE LEADERSHIP STYLE

Select a leadership style when creating a project office or leading any other change initiative. A continuum of approaches exists; options range from an Attila to a Quaker. Attila the Hun was a cruel and fearsome invader. The Attila leadership style represents top-down, command-and-control, standardized processes. The Quaker style, on the other hand, is bottom-up, gets results, and shows benefits—similar to how early Quakers reaped bountiful harvests and attracted attention from hungry Native Americans, thereby creating a pull effect rather than having to push others towards action. Attila is more competitive while Quaker is more collaborative.

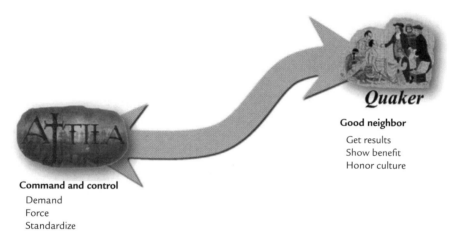

Quaker

Good neighbor

Get results
Show benefit
Honor culture

Command and control

Demand
Force
Standardize

FIGURE 11-1: Leadership Styles from Attila to Quaker

Any change initiative requires an influential sponsor. The Attila approach needs a higher-level person. In the Quaker approach, the sponsor's level is less important than his or her stature and breadth of influence.

The Quaker approach takes time and patience. A hybrid approach begins with the Quaker and moves toward the Attila model if necessary. Start with true believers who demonstrate, through small wins, the benefits of the change. This approach develops credibility. When a critical mass is "converted," apply a top-down command to convince the die-hards. This is a realistic approach for leading change in many organizations.

TOOLSET: THE CHANGE PROCESS

With acknowledgement of those who came before us, including Englund, Graham, and Dinsmore in *Creating the Project Office: A Manager's Guide to Leading Organizational Change* (2003), we connect the phases of change and change agent processes to the example of developing a project office (see Table 11-1).

TABLE 11-1: Change Management Phases

Change Phase	Change Agent Processes	Project Office Development
Create conditions for change	Establish a sense of urgency	Benchmarking (continual function); organizational vision; identify challenges and/or business opportunities; form a value proposition
	Develop political acumen	Do stakeholder analysis; identify political forces; develop political plan
	Create a guiding coalition	Line up supporters; convene PM council with organization-wide representation; recruit powerful executive sponsor
	Develop a vision and strategy	Craft PM office vision, what it will do—clear, convincing, compelling, concise Decide strategy, start small, expand with success
	Communicate the change vision	Meet with all organization constituents; generate enthusiasm

Make change happen	Generate short-term wins	Apply standard process to immediate problem; show value
	Develop broad-based action	Develop constituency through training, mentoring, consulting, developing a career path; expand offerings
	Consolidate gains and produce more change	Reorganize to establish a chief project officer Change reward system; develop portfolio management and venture project management system
Make change stick	Make project management the norm	Change organizational culture by providing leadership, learning, means, and the motivation to make the change the new reality

TOOLSET: SPECIFICATION CHANGE MANAGEMENT

Figure 11-2 illustrates an example of a specification change process that draws most elements of change management and change control together. The management aspect is getting people to accept and use the process. Control is ensuring only the right changes are made—and made right.

A specification change process like this may be needed because:

- There are problems with specification changes across the organization
  - Changes are being made without notification.
  - There is a presumption that a change will be made, but it is not.
- An agreed-upon process brings stability and flexibility.

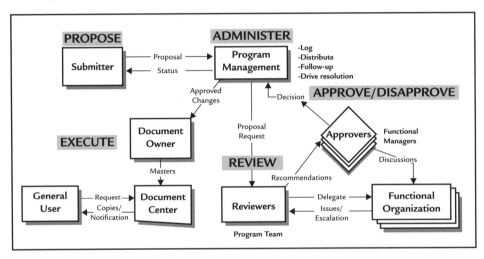

FIGURE 11-2: Specification Change Management Process

Good processes ensure that key people across an organization review the impact of proposed changes and that all people have access to the status of change requests and are informed when changes occur. Some changes are positive and are necessary for organizations that need to be flexibly innovative, so the process seeks not just to minimize changes but to assess and efficiently implement necessary changes.

Effective leadership is needed to proactively anticipate and manage not only the process aspects of change control but also the people issues involved in change management.

TOOLSET: TESTIMONIALS ON THE PROCESS OF CHANGE

Ryan Donahue, VP of software development and a software architect for StudyManager Inc, has been architecting and developing software for over 15 years; much of his experience is specific to software for clinical trials and health IT. Here is his experience with a change process:

> A couple of years ago my organization, which produces enterprise software for health IT, made a decision to change our software development method from a traditional waterfall method to an agile scrum method. This change was initiated by the product team, which I lead. The agile scrum method has multiple principles that define it. Some of these principles required the organization to make drastic changes in how we functioned. One example of such a principle is that software development is worked on incrementally and has consent review by a diverse group of stakeholders. In our case the stakeholders included the traditional product team (software developers, testers, product managers), but also included representatives from our customer support, customer project management, and sales teams, and in some cases customers themselves.
>
> The change to require stakeholders to be part of the development process was very difficult for some of my team members and other individuals within the organization. Some of the software developers felt that having others doing consent review of their work was putting them in an unfair position where they would always be "put on the spot" and be under intense pressure to perform. In addition they felt that it would be like having "multiple bosses" to answer to. On the other side, some of the stakeholders from other teams felt that having to review the work, provide input and feedback, and complete tasks related to the scrum process would be a large amount of work added to what they were already responsible for.
>
> After allowing everyone involved to voice their concerns, the sponsors of this change decided that the best approach was to take a small project and "try out" the new development method with the individuals who had concerns. This proved to be a success; stakeholders were able to see the benefits of the new method/change and realized that it added far less to their workload than they had thought. It gave them a forum in which the development work being done more closely met the expectations and needs of their customers, which actually reduced their overall workload.
>
> In addition, the software developers realized that they were able to remove a lot of frustrations about their work as the new review process allowed them to ask questions, bring up issues, get impediments removed,

and have a greater level of success in meeting the needs of the stakeholders and customers—which gave the developers an overall increase in their job satisfaction.

I do not think there were any significant ethical issues involved, and I'm not sure the situation could have been handled better. That said, I do feel that providing more information up front on the benefits of the change, and maybe providing case study information, would have helped reduce some of the perceived problems the change would bring.

A fellow student replied,

Hi Ryan,

Your sponsor took the right approach by trying out with a small project first. It is a great step towards change. By trying out a small project, one will meet less resistance and stakeholders will be more willing to accept changes, which is illustrated in your case. In our organization, the management also takes the approach of trying out changes at the department level first before implementing on the corporate level.

Christopher Pulliam, an applications coordinator with a government agency who works in an IT group that manages all organizational systems, says,

The *PMBOK Guide®* discusses change control as a set of processes involved in the Monitor and Control phases of the project. Process inputs for change control can come from forces internal and external to the project. How those changes are then considered and/or executed is the primary function of the change control process. But, it must also include making adjustments to documentation and other project assets after the change is implemented in an effort to be thorough and consistent.

Change control is the process portion of the overall change management within an organization. Even if the processes dictated in the project management plan and any separate organizational processes are followed, there may still be additional work to smoothly implement the change. Depending on the type of change, it's important to strive for as little behavioral and motivational fallout as possible. Changes that are presented poorly or suddenly can have ripple effects throughout the entire project.

Something that really clicked for me is the concept of the project manager as an "agent of change." I found this to be very helpful both in the context of a project as well as in the context of the organization overall. The term "project manager" up until this point made me conceptualize just another manager, making decisions and being the authority on issues that are presented. This doesn't prevent the PM from being a good manager, but conceptualizing a PM as a "change agent" does a great job of expanding his/her role. Looking at it from that perspective pushes you to develop mechanisms that can lead the project and organization down a desired path. These mechanisms can be both active and passive.

In dealing with change, I think the more passive mechanisms and processes that are built in, the more project team members can feel like they are operating as a team within a set environment ("Quaker"-style). The more active processes there are (such as after-the-fact directives from management), the more the team is likely to feel an "Attila"-type management experience. If the PM works hard to understand the motivations and personalities of the team members, then he/she is able to guide the project team in a more organic manner. That isn't to say that the same direction could not be achieved via an "Attila"-type, command-and-control approach. However, I think it's been proven that shifting towards more of a "Quaker" style tends to yield better results overall.

I also see this concept feeding into the idea of the PM as a "host" rather than a "hero." It should be the PM's job to create an environment where smart/capable workers are given the ability to buy in to changes and decisions being made throughout a project. A "hero" would want to be responsible for all decisions (large and small) based strictly on his/her individual judgment.

Within my own organization, we have a fairly strict command-and-control type of leadership approach. But because of our business, it's for good reason and will not likely change. Within our own IT group, though, we have adopted a much more "Quaker" type leadership approach. Even though some of the staff have more senior positions than others, we constantly strive to get input from others and rarely act independently if there is steadfast disagreement among the group.

Management does occasionally ask for suggestions when it comes to change. Sometimes it seems to be to placate members of the team, whereas other times it will be taken more seriously. However, a majority of the time our suggestions (in relation to change or anything else) need to be routed through our direct supervisor. So we find that the key message behind our suggestions can get lost, shifted, or deemphasized, which I think is a general frustration. So when we're asked directly by higher management for our feedback in a meeting or in the hallway, those are the moments the members of our group tend to seize upon.

It does seem like living with a Quaker-style approach in the day-to-day decisions would make the larger Attila decisions a little easier to deal with.

TOOLSET: *ALICE IN WONDERLAND* AS CHANGE AGENT

Watch the movie trailer for the 2010 version of this classic story. Note how these words describe both Alice and the actress who portrays her as a complete project manager:

Curious and curiouser…
It's a completely new story.
Alice returning; no longer 10 but 18 [years old].
Since she's been gone, the Red Queen has taken over Wonderland.
Alice comes across wild characters.
Becomes part of force fighting oppression of Red Queen
Heroine has to step up in a new way she never expected…and save the day.
We have our champion.
You are Alice; I'd know you anywhere.

Mia is incredible, perfect for the role.
Needed somebody that has a gravity to them; Mia had a quality of being both a young and an old soul at the same time.
Her experience is finding herself again.
Finding that she has the strength to be more self-assured.

He wouldn't be there if it weren't for me.
From the moment I fell down that rabbit hole, I've been told
what I must do,
who I must be.
I've been shrunk, stretched, scratched
And stuffed into a teapot.
I've been accused of being Alice, and of not being Alice.
But this is my path; I'll decide where it goes from here.
I make the path.

This is impossible.
Only if you believe it is.
This is only a dream; nothing can hurt me.
Oh yea.

MARKET AND CUSTOMER KNOWLEDGE

TOOLSET: COMPETITIVE ANALYSIS

The necessary steps for competitive analysis consist of identifying a list of competitors, understanding who the competitors are, keeping up with competitors' technological developments, and identifying what or where new competitors will come from.

1. **Draw up a list of competitors.** The content of that list will depend on how you define the market in the first place. For example, if you are in the project management consulting business, your competitors would be the big three PM consulting providers in a particular country.

2. **Who are the competitors?** Your core team members need to agree on who your competitors are and assign somebody to monitor specific competitors' actions. When you assign people to monitor competitors, you will probably be surprised by the large volume of news that they will gather.

3. **Keep up with competitors' technological developments.** Understanding competitors' developments is crucial for project success. This information will allow you to assess whether current developments are sufficient and what trends will guide the market in the future.

4. **Identify what new competitors might look like.** If you were going to start a new firm to compete with the outcome of your project, what would you do? Armed with this information, you can begin to monitor the business strategies of your competition. Some questions that need to be answered are:
   - What is your competitor's strategy?
   - What is their competitive advantage?
   - Are they lowering prices, increasing service levels, adding features...?
   - How do you think your competitors will respond to your service offerings?

TOOLSET: MARKETING TASKS

We propose that complete project managers attend to the following marketing tasks throughout the project life cycle. Some of these tasks may be accomplished by a marketing person on the core team or a business analyst. By default, however, the project manager needs to ensure that these tasks are addressed on every project.

At project initiation:

- Communicate with customers and end users; talk to them, ask questions
- Define initial definitions of product specifications and functions
- Define market and market size and potential sales volume
- Understand who your competitors are and their reactions
- Define concept life cycle and product life cycle
- Use prototyping to get more end-user inputs on what they need.

At project planning:

- Talk to customers and end users
- Define initial product specifications
- Evaluate competitor actions
- Assess customer demand
- Estimate market share and sales volume
- Define price points
- Refine product life cycle.

At project execution and control:

- Continue talking to customers and end users
- Change product specifications as needed
- Monitor competitor reactions
- Define price.

At project closing:

- Continue talking to customers and end users
- Launch product
- Operate and evaluate
- Support marketing and sales

- Look for opportunities for improvement
- Record what you learned.

Throughout a product's market life cycle:
- Monitor whether proposed benefits are being achieved
- Form new business cases based on observations
- Maintain productive relationships with customers and end users.

TOOLSET: EXEMPLARY CLIENT SPONSORSHIP— CASE STUDY

Aspects of working with customers and client sponsors are illustrated by a case study, that of my (Bucero) experience working as a PM consultant with a Spanish logistics company in Barcelona. The customer business focused on operations, but they needed to manage many projects in order to improve their operations. The customer had five technical project managers in the engineering department who had been managing projects without any methodology for years. So the management decided to hire Bucero PM Consulting to make an assessment in order to understand their culture and propose some changes if needed.

I used the Environmental Assessment Survey Instrument (EASI) from my colleague Englund and assessed the customer environment by interviewing 25 people from various positions in the organization. I also reviewed ten of the projects they managed. I found very little documentation and discipline in most of them. After running that evaluation, I presented an assessment report with my recommendations to the management team. My first recommendation was that they needed to make some changes. I convinced the management team as to the urgency of those changes. The proposed changes were:

- Train the organization in project management basics
- Define, write, and communicate to the whole organization clear roles and responsibilities for the project manager, sponsor, team, and customer
- Develop a customized PM methodology according to customer project types
- Help the organization implement that methodology.

It took more than two months to convince them that they needed those changes. When they finally agreed, I explained that those activities were part of a "change management project" and that I needed a project sponsor and a team assigned to that critical project. I would act as a project manager.

The project sponsor was the managing director for the customer. He is a very busy person, but he always was very supportive in terms of reinforcing my words in front of the management team, project managers, and other stakeholders. I worked with him and his management team to prepare an executive presentation for the rest of the managers, in order to explain the meaning of project management and how the way of managing projects in their organization would need to change. I sat down with him periodically and prepared a communication plan in order to maintain communications throughout the whole project life cycle.

I created an internal newsletter to inform all people in the organization about the evolution of the project. He pushed for and always supported the publication of that monthly newsletter. I asked him to present to the board of directors the definitions of the main roles defined in their PM methodology for approval and review, and he did it. He always was confident in my advice and best practices, reinforcing them in front of his people. He showed up regularly and was very open and talkative with people all the time.

At the end of the project, all members of the organization had been trained, and the whole management team understood what project management means and how it could help them be more successful and effective in their operations through projects. The PM methodology was developed and moved into the implementation phase.

The cultural change is taking much effort from everybody in the organization (mainly customer and project managers) but also from the management level. The level of commitment, trust, openness, accessibility, authenticity, and integrity of the managing director of this company has been exemplary. He is still ready to listen to me and learn from and support me. In fact, he proposed me as a project manager for one of the biggest projects the organization needed to manage in Barcelona.

TOOLSET: THE SCRAPPY PROJECT MANAGEMENT CHECKLIST

Kimberly Wiefling is a force of nature who seems to be on a relentless quest not only to survive the messiness of nature but to prosper. She is a globally recognized author and business leadership consultant who specializes in helping people achieve what seems impossible but is merely difficult. To help complete project managers everywhere, we asked Kimberly to summarize her popular book, *Scrappy Project Management—The 12 Predictable and Avoidable Pitfalls Every Project Faces* (2007).

Scrappy means not relying on a title to be a leader, being willing to take chances, take risks, and put yourself out there in order to do the right thing. Scrappy means having the steely resolve of a street fighter when necessary, being willing to be scared while sticking to your guns, being committed beyond confidence and ability, committed to making a difference. Scrappy means focusing on creating something extraordinary more than worrying about social acceptance and the approval of others. Scrappy is EDGY!

Scrappy project managers don't settle for hysterics and management by crisis, and they certainly don't let something as mundane as so-called reality limit them. They either find a way to seize success from the snapping jaws of defeat, or they invent one. This checklist will help you get results when the odds are against you, when precedence says it can't be done, and when the majority of humans believe your project is impossible.

I know a pilot who has flown 7,000 hours. The other day I asked him, "Chuck, the next time you fly, are you going to use your pre-flight checklist?" "You bet!" he replied. Now why would a jet pilot with that much experience use a checklist? Because that's what professionals do. Professionals know that in the heat of battle, much of our blood rushes to our arms and legs, where it is useful for hitting, kicking, and running, leaving little to nourish the one major advantage that we have over monkeys—our frontal lobes. That's why these commonsense principles are those that are most frequently overlooked or shortchanged on projects, even by those who should know better.

A checklist, or a set of operating guidelines, is one way to instill this kind of discipline. It's a rock in a sea of flotsam and jetsam. It's the next best thing to being lucky. Keep it with you at all times. Make a copy to nail up to the wall of your office. Tape another copy to the dashboard of your car, and put yet another on the lower surface of your favorite toilet seat so you'll be sure to see it at least a couple of times a day. And don't use mine, for Pete's sake! Make one that's your very own that suits you.

Knowing "how," all by itself, has never been enough to change anything. Smarter and more experienced people than us have tumbled down the stairs of failure due to overlooking exactly these basics. I've been using this list of operating principles for years to guide me through treacherous waters. It has helped me remember what's important when I'm not thinking straight. I don't follow it precisely, of course, but at least when I depart from it I do so thoughtfully, not by accidentally forgetting some important part of the project management process.

The converse of the dirty dozen are twelve commonsense practices for project management that have been proven to enable leaders to steer their teams clear of avoidable disaster and as much as double their chances of project success.

The role of project leader is not for the faint of heart. As in many worthy causes, tact and diplomacy can only get you so far, so be sure to have some spunk and attitude on hand when you run out of road with the gentler approach. Sometimes an outrageous act of bravado and nerves of steel will serve you far better than any fancy-schmancy Microsoft Project Gantt chart. It is during these defining moments that you'll come to appreciate and benefit from the scrappy approach to leading a project, and this handy-dandy checklist. Don't leave home without it!

The 12 Predictable and Avoidable Pitfalls Every Project Faces

If you're genetically gifted with the ability to get results that other people claim are highly unlikely or darn near impossible, you don't need this checklist. But if you are faced with an insurmountable to-do list, here are twelve predictable—and avoidable—pitfalls that stand between most people and the goals they hope to achieve for success:

1. **Forget about the customer.** Henry Ford said that the company doesn't pay employees a salary, the customer does. The employer is just the middleman. But many businesses operate as though the customer is an afterthought. One trip to a retail service establishment is all it takes to confirm this. If you want to be successful, be completely and unrepentantly obsessed with the customer, whoever that is, whether internal or external.

2. **Fail to set clear goals.** According to a blizzard of studies, and my own observations of businesses over the past 20 years, the number-one reason people don't achieve their goals is that they don't have goals. Fear of failure helps people avoid clear goal-setting, or makes them settle for fuzzy, ambiguous goals. Double your chances of success just by making sure that you and your co-workers have shared, measurable, challenging, and achievable goals, as clear as sunlight.

3. **Communicate poorly.** Even with clear and compelling goals, inadequate communication undermines your chances of achieving those goals. Poor communication is the number-two cause of failure, and it's no wonder. Most people don't realize that communication involves both talking and listening. Many conversations are like two TVs facing one another. Highly successful people avoid this all-too-common pitfall by engaging in effective, vociferous, and unrelenting communication with all stakeholders.

4. **Keep roles and responsibilities fuzzy.** Fumbled handoffs and the left hand not knowing what the right hand is doing are common causes of setbacks along the road to success. One of the biggest causes of conflicts in teams is lack of role clarity. Assure that roles and responsibilities are clearly understood and agreed to by all to avoid this unnecessary pit stop on your journey.

5. **Plan inadequately and create fictitious schedules.** Every hour of planning saves about a day of wasted effort and rework. And yet, given a choice, most people will either underplan or fail to plan at all. Even when you create detailed schedules, they often do little more than document the demise of the people carrying out the plan. Overlooking critical hand-offs and interdependencies can add days, weeks, or months to the completion date of a mission-critical goal, and what's worse, everyone seems to know from the start the dates will never be met. Savvy professionals create viable plans and schedules that enjoy the team's hearty commitment.

6. **Imagine no disaster and see no upside.** Many people are so busy just working on the tasks at hand that they fail to look around the next bend for possible potholes that could have a major impact on their results. Even when risks are identified, the most common mistake is to do nothing to avoid them. And when you're up to your butt in alligators, the last thing you want to do is stop to consider how to make the outcome better! Those in the know mitigate big, hairy, abominable risks before they occur, and keep a keen lookout for upsides that can accelerate and amplify their success.

7. **Behave as if everything is the top priority.** If everything is number one, nothing is! Of course, we'd love to have it all, avoiding tough trade-offs between things we hold dear. But choices must inevitably be made. Sometimes costs need to increase in order to obtain a satisfactory level of quality. Sometimes features must be sacrificed in the name of reliability or to hit a hard deadline in a launch window. No one wants to lose one of their vital organs, but the reality is that sometimes you

must prioritize ruthlessly, choosing between heart, lungs, and kidneys if necessary.

8. **Be surprised when change occurs.** There isn't a project on earth that has been accomplished without some kind of change that impacted it. And yet people continue to let change throw them off balance. Change is inevitable, except from vending machines. Only amnesiacs should be surprised by it. The world is changing rapidly, and your projects are too, so anticipate and accommodate necessary and inevitable change.

9. **Fall victim to self-limiting assumptions.** Of all the obstacles we face in life, none are bigger than those of our own making. We fail to consider possibilities outside of our experience, or possibilities that, in the past, have been off-limits to us for some reason, like because we have self-limiting beliefs about what is possible. And, like fish blind to water, we miss opportunities right in front of our nose because of the filters of our experience. There are plenty of examples where people saying something was impossible were shoved aside by those doing it. Avoid this trap by routinely challenging assumptions and beliefs, especially insidious self-imposed limitations.

10. **Fail to manage stakeholder expectations.** What is a stakeholder? Anyone who cares about what you're doing, and anyone who can either help you or hurt you in your quest to achieve your goals. Most people fail to identify key stakeholders who could dramatically accelerate or undermine their success. A powerful stakeholder analysis tool that clarifies goals is a stakeholder map. After visualizing all stakeholders and their interrelationships, ask, "What will this stakeholder be saying when this project is wildly successful?" Frequently, expectations will conflict, forcing to the surface the tough decisions and trade-offs between things that initially seemed equally important. Managing the expectations of all stakeholders up front increases the likelihood that your delight in accomplishing your goals will be shared by others who are critical to your process.

11. **Repeat the mistakes of the past.** A common practice among professionals is to do what's called a "retrospective," where things that went well, and those that went sideways, are reviewed with the intention of avoiding similar problems in the future. However, like a B-grade horror flick, the mistakes look pretty much the same each time through. That's why I call these reviews "lessons *not* learned." There's a difference between ten years of experience and one year of experience ten times. Learn from experience. Make new and more exciting mistakes each time!

12. **Skip being grateful for what's going right.** We seem to be condi-
tioned from an early age to notice what's not working and focus on criticism instead of appreciation for what's right with the world and other
people. And that bias toward critique is reinforced by a society where
negative people appear smarter. Recognizing what's working well is
equally important. Appreciating our contributions and those of others provides much needed motivation to continue onward. Even mistakes can open a doorway to new possibilities, especially in the world of
creativity and innovation. Post-It notes were an accident—a failure of
stickiness. Practice an attitude of gratitude. If you want to truly achieve
your greatest potential, celebrate successes along the way—and some
failures, too!

Scrappy Project Management Checklist
- Be completely and unrepentantly obsessed with the "customer."
- Prioritize ruthlessly, choosing between heart, lungs, and kidneys if
  necessary.
- Provide shared, measurable, challenging, and achievable goals as clear
  as sunlight.
- Create viable plans and schedules that enjoy the team's hearty
  commitment.
- Explicitly identify and plan to mitigate detestable risks and delectable
  accelerators.
- Assure that roles and responsibilities are unmistakably understood and
  agreed by all.
- Challenge assumptions and beliefs, especially insidious self-imposed
  limitations.
- Manage the expectations of all stakeholders: underpromise and
  overdeliver.
- Anticipate and accommodate necessary and inevitable change.
- Engage in effective, vociferous, and unrelenting communication with
  all stakeholders.
- Practice an "attitude of gratitude." Celebrate success, and some fail-
  ures, too.
- Learn from experience. Make new and more exciting mistakes next time!

Feeling lucky? Play the lottery. But if you want to generate positive results
predictably and reliably, follow these practical and sensible guidelines
for getting things done. Heeding these land mines on the path to success
doesn't guarantee success, but at least you'll fail for new, surprising, and
more exciting reasons. Cling to the Scrappy Project Management Checklist
as if your success depends on it . . . because indeed it does!

The next time you're looking down the barrel of another killer project, pause and reflect before diving into the fray. In the middle of the madness, surface for a look around before diving into the pile of work that awaits you. And cling to what you know works. A set of operating principles like those above can be a useful reminder of key areas that are important to the success of the mammals on your team. Follow the principles or depart from them thoughtfully, no matter how you feel at the moment. Professional project leaders do what needs to be done whether or not they feel like it. Not everyone will like this kind of disciplined approach. Be strong and keep it scrappy!

APPENDIX

We offer this short assessment tool as a starting point for the journey to becoming a complete project manager. Visit www.englundpmc.com and www.abucero.com for this and other toolsets.

Skill	Novice	Project Manager	Complete Project Manager	Uber Project Manager
Leadership/ management	• Doesn't rec-ognize need • Gets lost • Loses track of time	• Aware	• Competent • Effective rela-tional chemistry • Courageous	• Extraordinary
Humor	• None	• Aware	• Makes fun a priority	• Always takes advantage of humor for project success
Personal	• Poor example	• Minimal respect	• Positive attitude • Influential • Passionate, persistent, and patient	• Charismatic

Project	• "What's a project?"	• Aware	• Competent in PM methodology • Uses best practices	• Program manager extraordinaire
Environment	• Chaotic	• Aware	• Creates project-friendly environment • Embraces chaos • Flexible	• Fun • Productive • Streamlined • Optimized
Organization	• Unaware	• Aware	• Culturally aware • "Green," not "toxic"	• Totally green
Negotiating	• Ignores	• Reluctant	• Prepares well • Focus on P^2O^2 • Asks for more	• Gets every-thing asked for
Political	• Naïve or shark • Victim	• Resistant	• Creates positive politics • Develops political plan • Credible	• Politically savvy
Conflict management	• Stressed	• Comfortable	• Constructive contention • Resolves productively	• Always resolves conflict proactively
Sales	• Ignores	• Resists	• Confident with objections • Good presenter • Gets commitments	• A winner
Change management	• Resists	• Accepts	• Ready to change • Manages change • Flexible	• Embraces change

Market and customer knowledge	• Avoids	• Accepts	• Researches customer and end-user needs • Aware of market forces • Maintain ethical relationships • Servant leader	• Loved by all he/she works with

Use this checklist as well as the molecular assessment chart in the Introduction as periodic reminders of progress (or setbacks) toward achieving completeness. Revel in your role as a leader and manager of project-based work. Best wishes on all your projects!

REFERENCES AND RESOURCES

Bolman, Lee G., and Terrence E. Deal (1997). *Reframing Organizations: Artistry, Choice, and Leadership*. 2nd ed. San Francisco: Jossey-Bass.

Bowles, Michelle (2011). "Getting the Green Light." *PM Network* (July): 45. http://www.pmi.org/en/Knowledge-Center/~/media/PDF/Publications/PMN0711%20Greenlight_fullstory.ashx (accessed November 2011).

Bucero, Alfonso (2010). *Today Is a Good Day! Attitudes for Achieving Project Success*. Oshawa, Ontario: Multi-Media Publications Inc.

Bucero, Alfonso, and Randall Englund (2006). "Building the Project Manager's Credibility: A Real Case Study." In *PMI Global Congress EMEA Proceedings*, Madrid, Spain.

Buckholtz, Thomas J. (2007). *Innovate Incisively: Gain Impact. Save Time.* Thomas J. Buckholtz.

——— (2011). "Metrics That Matter: Measuring and Improving the Value of Service." In *Service Systems Implementation*, edited by Haluk Demirkan, James C. Spohrer, and Vikas Krishna. Service Science: Research and Innovation in the Service Economy. New York: Springer Science+Business Media. DOI 10.1007/978-1-4419-7904-9_13.

Byrne, John A. (2003). "How to Lead Now." *Fast Company* (August): 62–70.

Cialdini, Robert B. (2000). *Influence: Science and Practice*. 4th ed. New York: Pearson, Allyn, & Bacon.

Cooperrider, David L., and Diana Whitney (2000). *Appreciative Inquiry: A Positive Revolution in Change*. San Francisco. Berrett-Koehler Publishers, Inc.

Covey, Stephen R., A. Roger Merrill, and Rebecca R. Merrill (1994). *First Things First*. New York: Simon & Schuster.

Czegledi, Jim (2011). "Your Sense of Humour, a Soft Skill for Hard Times." PMI Government Community of Practice newsletter (October): 8–14.

DeCarlo, Doug (2001). "Traditional Project Management vs. Extreme Project Management." ProjectConnections. http://www.projectconnections.com/articles/070901-decarlo.html (accessed December 2011).

Englund, Randall (2004). "Leading with Power." Presentation at the PMI Global Congress North America, Anaheim, California.

Englund, Randall L. (2009). "Applying Chaos Theory in a Project-Based Organization." Presentation at the PMI Congress EMEA, Amsterdam. http://blog.projectconnections.com/project_practitioners/2009/05/applying-chaos-theory-in-a-project-based-organization.html (accessed December 2011).

———— (2010). "Ten Rules of Negotiating." http://englundpmc.com/offerings%20page.htm (accessed December 2011).

————. Political Plan slides and templates. http://www.englundpmc.com/Creating%20Poli%20Plan_re.pdf (accessed December 2011).

————. "Speaking Truth to Power: Leading from the Middle to Correct a Troubled Architecture." http://www.projectconnections.com/interviews/detail/case-speaking-truth-to-power.html (accessed December 2011).

Englund, Randall L., and Alfonso Bucero (2006). *Project Sponsorship: Achieving Management Commitment for Project Success*. San Francisco: Jossey-Bass Publishers.

Englund, Randall L., Robert J. Graham, and Paul Dinsmore (2003). *Creating the Project Office: a Manager's Guide to Leading Organizational Change*. San Francisco: Jossey-Bass.

Englund, Randall L., and Ralf Müller (2004). "Leading Change Towards Enterprise Project Management." *Projects & Profits* (November).

Esque, Timm (1999). *No Surprises Project Management*. Ensemble Management Consulting.

Eubanks, David (2010). *How to Be a Project Manager without Getting Killed*. CreateSpace.

Examiner (2009). "What Shade of Green Are You?" March 15, p. 5.

Fisher, Roger, and William Ury (1981). *Getting to Yes: Negotiating Agreement Without Giving In*. New York: Houghton Mifflin.

Frame, J. Davidson (1999). *Building Project Management Competence*. San Francisco: Jossey-Bass.

Gladwell, Malcolm (2002). *The Tipping Point: How Little Things Can Make a Big Difference*. Boston: Back Bay Books.

Goleman, Daniel, Richard Boyatzis, and Annie McKee. (2002). *Primal Leadership: Realizing the Power of Emotional Intelligence*. Boston: Harvard Business School Press.

Heerkens, Gary R. (2011). "Executives Aren't the Only Ones Who Should Be Business-Savvy." *PM Network* (July): 17.

Kouzes, James M., and Barry Z. Posner (2007). *The Leadership Challenge*. 4th ed. San Francisco: Jossey-Bass.

Langley, Mark (2011). *PMI Today* (July): p. 10.

Lauridsen, Robert W., and Steven J. Sherman (2000). *Boss Talk … A Manager's Guide to Exceptional Productivity and Innovation*. London/Warner Publishing.

Levine, Michael (1996). *Bottom Line/Personal* (May 15): 12.

Mourkogiannis, Nikos (2008). *Purpose: The Starting Point of Great Companies*. New York: Palgrave Macmillan.

O'Brochta, Michael (2011). "How to Accelerate Executive Support for Projects." Paper presented at PMI EMEA Congress, Dublin, Ireland.

O'Connor, Paul (2011). "Irrational Portfolio Management." The Adept Group eNewsletter (January 31). www.adept-plm.com.

Phillips, Michael, and Salli Rasberry (1974). *The Seven Laws of Money*. San Francisco: Clear Glass Publications.

Pinto, José (2011). Organizational Project Management Community of Practice newsletter (November).

"Projector Humor." Retrieved from http://www.hpitnewsletters.com/projectorhumor.html.

Rothman, Jay (1997). *Resolving Identity-Based Conflict in Nations, Organizations, and Communities*. San Francisco: Jossey-Bass.

Russell, Lou (2003). *Learning Flash* email newsletter (August).

Senge, Peter M. (2006). *The Fifth Discipline: The Art & Practice of the Learning Organization*. New York: Crown Business.

Shelley, Arther (2009). Being a Successful Knowledge Leader. Ark Group.

———— (2006). The Organizational Zoo: A Survival Guide to Work Place Behavior. Asian Publishing.

Somani, Sheilina (2011). *PM Network* (April): 20.

Swanson, Sandra A. (2011). "The Basics of Six Sigma". *PM Network* (July): 57–58.

"SWOT Analysis." http://www.learning3pointzero.com/wp-content/uploads/2011/01/swot_img2.gif (accessed December 2011).

Toppenberg, Gustav (2011)."What's the Color of the Sky in Your Project World?" http://svprojectmanagement.com/what%E2%80%99s-the-color-of-the-sky-in-your-project-world (accessed December 2011).

U.S. Department of Education, Office of Planning, Evaluation, and Policy Development (2010). *Evaluation of Evidence-Based Practices in Online Learning: A Meta-Analysis and Review of Online Learning Studies*. Washington, D.C: U.S. Department of Education.

Wiefling, Kimberly (2007). *Scrappy Project Management: The 12 Predictable and Avoidable Pitfalls Every Project Faces*. Silicon Valley, CA: Happy About.

Wong, Zachary A. (2007). *Human Factors in Project Management: Concepts, Tools, and Techniques for Inspiring Teamwork and Motivation*. San Francisco: Jossey-Bass.

Complement Your Project Management Library with These Additional Resources from

MANAGEMENTCONCEPTPRESS

The Complete Project Manager: Integrating People, Organizational, and Technical Skills
Randall Englund and Alfonso Bucero

This bookintegrates theory and application, humor and passion, and concepts and examples drawn from the authors' experiences as well as from contributors who share their stories. The concepts are easy to understand, universal, powerful, and readily applicable. There is no complicated model to understand before practicing what you learn...or wish you had learned when starting your career.

ISBN 978-1-56726-359-6 ■ Product Code B596 ■ 286 pages

The Project Management Coaching Workbook: Six Steps to Unleashing Your Potential
Susanne Madsen

Starting with an insightful self-assessment, this book offers tools, questions, reviews, guiding practices, and exercises that will help you build your roadmap to project management and leadership success.Based on her experience as a coach and mentor, Susanne Madsen offers a proven six-step method designed to help you understand and articulate what you want to achieve—and then assist you in achieving those goals.

ISBN 978-1-56726-357-2 ■ Product Code B572 ■ 236 pages

Interpersonal Skills for Portfolio, Program, and Project Managers
Ginger Levin, DPA, PMP, PgMP

Any formula for management success must include a high level of interpersonal skills. The growing complexity of organizational portfolios, programs, and projects, as well as the increasing number and geographic dispersion of stakeholders and employees, makes a manager's interpersonal skills critical. The frequency and variety of interpersonal interactions and the pressure to perform multiple leadership roles successfully while ensuring customer satisfaction have never been greater. This book offers practical and proven tools and methods you can use to develop your interpersonal skills and meet the challenges of today's competitive professional environment.

ISBN 978-1-56726-288-9 ■ Product Code B889 ■ 286 pages

The Project Management Answer Book
Jeff Furman, PMP

This easy-to-use Q&A reference covers all aspects of project management and includes practical tips on obtaining the PMP and related certifications. This book provides you with the tools you need to improve project performance and achieve high-quality, low-risk results immediately.

ISBN 978-1-56726-297-1 ■ Product Code B971 ■ 416 pages

Guerrilla Project Management
Kenneth T. Hanley

This book emphasizes key project management competencies, including managing stakeholders effectively, assessing risk accurately, and getting agreement on the objective measures of project success. Focusing on these and other competencies as well as effective PM processes and tools, Hanley presents an alternative approach to project management that is light, fast, and flexible — and adapts readily to the many changes every project manager faces.

ISBN 978-1-56726-294-0 ■ Product Code B940 ■ 236 pages

Project Team Dynamics:
Enhancing Performance, Improving Results
Lisa DiTullio

The author clearly outlines methods for creating and implementing a structure to deal with the inevitable difficulties that any team may encounter. With examples drawn from contemporary project management, she demonstrates the effectiveness of this straightforward approach and highlights the risks of not building a strong team culture.

ISBN 978-1-56726-290-2 ■ Product Code B902 ■ 179 pages

The 77 Deadly Sins of Project Management

In this book, the contributors focus on each "deadly sin" and probe its manifestations and consequences for projects. By sharing their personal experiences, as well as some historical events, the contributors spotlight the effects and costs — both financial and human — of failing to get a handle on these sins and reign them in. Through anecdotes and case studies, this book will help you better understand how to execute the myriad aspects of today's projects.

ISBN 978-1-56726-246-9 ■ Product Code B777 ■ 357 pages

Project Management Fundamentals:
Key Concepts and Methodologies, Second Edition
Gregory T. Haugan, PhD, PMP

This completely revised edition offers new project managers a solid foundation in the basics of the discipline. Using a step-by-step approach and conventional project management (PM) terminology, *Project Management Fundamentals* is a commonsense guide that focuses on how essential PM methods, tools, and techniques can be put into practice immediately.

ISBN 978-1-56726-281-0 ■ Product Code B810 ■ 380 pages

Order today for a 30-day risk-free trial!
Visit www.managementconcepts.com/pubs or call 800-506-4450

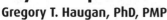